Praise for *Moo*

MU00714058

Moon Over Cabarete will appeal to many different audiences—Caribbean travelers, expats, and retirees who enjoy observations about economic changes in developing countries. This is a story of hopes and losses told with humor and affection.

—Lynn Rockwell, *Red-hot Proofreading*

Moon Over Cabarete is a personal and endearing account of societal change over a score of years, as commerce and technology transform the day to day life in a quaint fishing village in the Dominican Republic—all seen through the eyes of an American couple, viewed with gusto and passion.

—Joseph Kaplan, *Literary Reviews*

Moon Over Cabarete is as much a love story as it is the humorous and sometimes bittersweet adventures of a New England couple pursuing their dreams in a foreign land; a modern day Innocents Abroad.

—Jesse McGuire, *South Pasadena Book Club*

Moon Over Cabarete is an engaging story full of anecdotes that have you smiling and shaking your head at the experiences of four friends living in a culture where they don't speak the language or know how things were done.

—Barbara DeWall, *Arizona Review*

MOON
OVER
CABARETE

A Travel Memoir of the Dominican Republic

Moon Over Cabarete

Published by Piscataqua Press

An imprint of RiverRun Bookstore

142 Fleet St.

Portsmouth, NH 03801

www.piscataquapress.com

ISBN: 978-1-939739-70-4

Author Website: www.juliebiggveazey.com

Printed in the United States of America

Cover Photo: Shutter stock/EDITHA

MOON OVER CABARETE

JULIE BIGG VEAZEY

with

BILL VEAZEY

ill and I are a second marriage. In mid-forties, we fell in love; a joy I r imagined would come to me again. with three teenagers in tow, mindful eir different personalities and needs, id our best to blend our families and see them through college. And then, it was our turn to follow our passions, to build our friendship, to approach each adventure extravagantly and romantically.

Join us in our travels on Facebook to view photos illustrating the events in *Moon Over Cabarete.*

www.facebook.com/moonovercabarete

To my daughter, Julie B.

who advocated, coaxed, cajoled, encouraged, goaded, pushed, urged, prompted, provoked, inspired, insisted, and persuaded until the only way we could make her stop was to write this book.

*Twenty years from now you will be
more disappointed by the things that you
didn't do than by the ones you did do. So
throw off the bowlines. Sail away from
the safe harbor. Catch the trade winds in
your sails. Explore. Dream. Discover.*

—Mark Twain

UNO

1987 - DISCOVERING CABARETE

Why did Bill and I find ourselves on a plane heading for the Dominican Republic one freezing February morning in 1987?

Ann and John, friends since forever, called right after they returned to their home in Massachusetts having just spent a sultry August weekend with us at our cottage on Merrymeeting Lake in New Hampshire. Between laughs and countless rehashing of past adventures shared, they had joined us in learning how to windsurf. It was a fairly new water sport at that time, where you'd stand on a sailboard measuring about two feet by ten feet, control the sail boom by hand, rotating it outward to go downwind, and pulling it in to close haul—all the time trying to stand upright on the board. We found that it wasn't easy teaching ourselves as we continually lost our balance and plunged into the lake. But it was energizing and we gained some measure of confidence by the end of the weekend.

"Hey, Bill," I yelled, "it's Ann and John on the phone. Pick up. They're all excited about an article in the *Boston Globe's* travel section about some little fishing village in the Dominican Republic."

John's voice enthused through the phone: "The author wrote

that Cabarete is located on the northern shore of the Dominican Republic, it's called the Amber Coast. And, among other things, (here, he paused dramatically) the new sport called *windsurfing* was just taking hold there."

"It's not a tourist trap," Ann said, "just a small, undeveloped village of only a couple of thousand Dominicans. The article raved about the simplicity of the place, and, wait till you hear this—all-you-can-eat at a place called *Mamita's* for 20-pesos, served on the patio of her home."

"I already looked it up." John quickly added, "That's about three dollars."

"So, let's go check it out," they shouted through two extensions, and on our end of the line, we responded: "Is there political unrest there?"

They answered in unison: "Oh, for heaven's sake . . ."

So, without further ado, we said: "Okay, count us in."

The minute we hung up, I rushed to look it up: *The Dominican Republic occupies the eastern two-thirds of Hispaniola, an island that it shares with Haiti in the West Indies. Its capital, Santo Domingo, founded in 1496 by Christopher Columbus, is the oldest European settlement in the Western Hemisphere, and is 18,816 square miles.*

About twice the size of New Hampshire.

*   *   *

We had known Ann and John socially during our first marriages to others, but our foursome friendship didn't take off until 1975 when Ann schemed a meeting between her two divorced friends. On that fateful, rainy August day, Bill and I met in Ann and John's kitchen and essentially fell in love. We were married nine months later.

Once the four of us who were all working full time coordinated our vacation dates in February of 1987, our travel agent made round trip flight reservations from Boston to Puerto Plata. "You're on your own after that," she said. "I can't make hotel reservations in Cabarete." (Which, by the way, is pronounced: ca-bar-et-tay). We asked why, to which she replied that there was no telephone service there. Undaunted, we told her to book the flights.

When the February 1987 date arrived, we boarded the plane, going from near zero degrees in Boston to 87 degrees in the roughly four hours it took us to get there. Descending through occasional clouds, we had our first view of the Dominican Republic, and if you believe in initial impressions as an omen of things to come, this trip was the beginning of something truly special. The coppery green of the sugarcane fields stretched for miles, leading to a ridge of mountains and a cloudless sky beyond. As we approached the airport, the deep cerulean color of the ocean gave way to tones of lighter blue and then the aqua green that you see in those travel magazines in doctors' waiting rooms.

Most of the passengers were Dominicans who had stuffed bulging shopping bags filled with toys, sneakers, and jeans under their seats or shoved in the overhead compartments, all tied with bits of colored string or closed with a crisscrossing of masking tape. They cheered and clapped when we landed—a ritual we took an exuberant part in on all future visits to the DR.

We shuffled along with the crowd into the rural international airport where inbound travelers were greeted by a three-man *Merengue* band of two drums and a guitar. The players nodded and smiled broadly as Ann and I quickly got into the mood and danced our way toward them, each placing a dollar on their brightly painted tray. When we reached the tourist arrival room, we learned about an entry fee which was to be collected along with a short form we had to fill out. At the same time, rum punch in plastic cups was generously offered. By the time we had finished with the papers and passed through the line, I didn't mind that there was no air-conditioning and that birds were diving from above, occasionally pooping from the rafters.

There were no luggage carousels, only a vast pile of suitcases randomly tossed, in every size and color. As we worked our way through the chaos of island reception, at least a dozen young porters surrounded us just as we retrieved our luggage. They jockeyed for our business, grabbing at our suitcases, moving them forward toward the Customs table where the inspectors gave only a cursory glance, waving us through. Their Spanish was nothing like anything I had studied; it sounded rich and romantic, but spoken with the speed of a machine gun. We had been handing out dollar bills left and right, which, I didn't realize at the time, was an enormous tip. Two porters probably in their fifties, dressed in clean white shirts and genuine smiles, won the battle and ushered us out of the concrete building that stood open-faced to the road filled with taxi drivers hustling for a fare, all shouting, waving and honking. Without consideration of consequences because they all looked the same, we chose the rattletrap taxicab right in front of us. The rusted fenders and a cracked rear window didn't bother us since the driver appeared to be a good guy with a pleasant smile, and the tires weren't completely bald. Out in the 80 degree sun, the noonday heat rose and shimmered.

Struggling with my very rusty high school Spanish of not more than two or three dozen words, I said to the driver, "*Cabarete, por favor, señor,*" and off we went, squeezed into a cab with no AC and Merengue and/or Salsa music blaring from the radio. Hot air poured in through the windows, and my hair that I had gotten up extra early to wash and blow dry, was transformed into tiny corkscrew curls within minutes. This is the way it's going to be, I told myself. Having battled bad hair days all my life, I'd better get used to it.

There was one highway—I use the term loosely—which ran approximately two hundred miles along the entire northern coast of the Dominican Republic. It had potholes that a bicycle-built-for-two could easily disappear into. There were stones that bordered on being boulders used as fillers forming sandy drop-offs on either side of the road where the macadam had fallen away. My personal favorite safety feature—a small tree trunk sticking up out of an open manhole in the middle of the road indicating that the cover had gone missing.

The landscape seemed typically Caribbean with brilliant

green vegetation contrasting with the reddish earth, while above it all puffy clouds scuttled across the clear blue sky. We passed through several little villages that appeared desperately poor, yet people were dressed in colorful clothes and children played happily in front yards that were swept clean. I had the impression that everyone we saw was smiling and waving to us as we sped by. There was the mysterious smell of something burning that drifted through the open windows as we left the airport. We had only a fleeting glimpse of Sosúa, a small city along the way that appeared to be quite developed. With no seatbelts and at breakneck speed, our driver honked and passed every car on the road, making what we had been told was a forty-five minute trip, in twenty minutes flat. Ann and I clutched the edge of the seat and the boys had their hands on the roof to keep from banging their heads. If there were traffic laws, it seemed they were purely optional.

Of course we had no reservations, so when the driver pulled into Cabarete, Ann spotted a sign with the hotel name she had read about in the *Boston Globe* article. She screamed, John yelled, "That's it," and I called out to the driver: "*Pare aquí.*" The cabbie slammed on the brake in the middle of the road and we all lurched forward. Feeling shaky and greatly relieved, we got out. He pulled our luggage out of the trunk, set it by the side of the road, obviously pleased that we paid in US dollars. He pointed down a dark, narrow alleyway toward what looked like the hotel entrance, then got back in his cab and took off.

Lugging the suitcases (this was before the now standard built-in wheels) about a hundred feet down the shadowed alley, we came to a three-story stucco building on the right with about six rooms on the upper two floors. We passed through an arched entrance that opened up to a rather large lobby, open and airy with several brightly colored couches, chairs and a long bamboo registration counter. The opposite wall to the counter was a series of arched openings beyond which were dining tables set with pastel cloth tablecloths, place settings, and fresh flowers on every table. A full service bar, off to the left of a small in-ground swimming pool, offered deck chairs and lounges. Very pleasantly surprised and feeling better about Cabarete by the minute, we checked in.

Luckily, Auberge du Roy Hotel was run by a Canadian, Jean Laporte, *who spoke English* and who said he only had one room available with two double beds. "We'll take it," we chimed in unison, and then added, "That's fine," when he mentioned that the only bathroom was down the hall from our room.

I walked through the lobby out to the open terrace facing the water while Bill was signing us up for the room. The scene was incredible. There was a stretch of white sand beach as far as I could see with just a few people strolling in the shimmering end-of-day sun. In the distance, I could hear the endless percussion of the pitch and tumble of the ocean. On the horizon, there were bands of pink and lavender glowing across the wet sand. Daylight was dropping into deep indigo.

In the room we would share for the week, there were two windows hidden by brightly flowered drapes, which we opened immediately. One window faced out over a native village with a small group of colorful bantam chickens, pigs, and one lone rooster milling around the yard next to the hotel. From the other, there was the pristine beach and the beautiful waters of the Atlantic, although many referred to the ocean as the Caribbean. We quickly changed into shorts and went down to the outdoor bar next to the beach, immediately ordered *piña coladas,* and sucked them down like coconut frappes.

As stated in the *Boston Globe,* Laporte told us that he had "discovered" Cabarete three years before, and with an eye to the easterly trade winds running parallel to the beach and the protective reef that created a large basin, he recognized it as perfect conditions for what might become world-class boardsailing. So, he built the hotel, imported windsurfing equipment to rent out, and opened a pizza joint on the main road east of Auberge du Roy. He was currently advertising in several Canadian travel magazines.

"Tourism for the adventuresome is taking hold in Cabarete, thanks to me," he said, tilting back in his wooden chair with a satisfied gleam in his eyes. In less than three years, Laporte told us, he had organized the first Professional Windsurfing Association World Cup.

Dominicans *loved* his pizza, taught themselves how to make it, how to windsurf, and how to work in a hotel. We have found that most Dominicans like to work and took pride in whatever they did for a living, always showing up for work in freshly laundered clothes and an enthusiastic attitude.

Later, we strolled down the beach, wiggled our very pale toes in the ocean-damp sand, and stopped for another round of coladas at Ono's Bar. While we ate all of the pretzels in front of us, including those all the way down the bar, the bartender hacked open a fresh coconut with his machete, poured the milk and shaved the meat into a tall container—along with lots of rum and some secret ingredients—then shook the drink to the same rhythm of the Salsa music that was loud enough to make conversation almost impossible. The drink was so delicious, we had a second round. As the evening cooled, we stayed long enough to see the fiery sun sink into the ocean.

Now, with four *coladas* under our belts, we decided it was time to let go of the day. Back in our room, for some reason that escapes me now, we were talking about funerals.

"I want to go to my own memorial service," I had announced drunkenly, flopping onto my back in the middle of our very lumpy bed. "Otherwise, it's a waste for people to say nice things about you and you don't get to hear them."

As if on cue, Bill, Ann, and John started circling the bed, waving their arms in the air, saying such lovely accolades to me. We ended our first day in the DR in gales of laughter.

*   *   *

Our next-door neighbor woke us at dawn, strutting his stuff and crowing like any rooster worth his salt. We jumped into our bathing suits and dashed into the ocean for an early morning swim, then back to the hotel patio for breakfast of fresh papaya, pineapple, bananas, eggs, and Mangú—a Dominican staple food, part of the banana family, made of mashed, boiled, steamed or fried plantain, similar to potatoes. And, the blackest coffee, in which your spoon stood straight up.

While waiting for Laporte to help rig us up for windsurfing, we lounged around the rest of the morning on the gorgeous half-moon beach, reported to be one of the longest stretches of uninterrupted sandy beaches in the DR. The horseshoe-shaped bay, protected from the high seas by breakwater reefs and bathed year-round by easterly breezes, is over two kilometers long offering ideal conditions for windsurfing. We couldn't wait to try our luck.

It didn't take any time at all to realize that having learned the previous summer on a fresh water lake in New Hampshire did not prepare us for the pull of the tide and the ocean swells. We all spent most of the time falling off and climbing back onto the board. Ann and I ruined our new bathing suits sliding across the roughened surface of the board, which in those days was exceptionally wide—a saving grace for such novices.

When we finally gave up around three pm, dragging our sails and boards into shore, a young Dominican boy perhaps taking pity on the exhausted *Americanos*, told us in quite good English that beginners should only sail in the morning because progressive trade winds and thermal winds pick up around noon, and by mid afternoon, the waves break from three to six feet high.

Well, HELLO! Where was he when we needed him? And why

hadn't Laporte warned us?

So, we changed our sailing routine to mornings when the Cabarete bay's light winds let us practice and learn, while by noon, a warm 15 to 20 knot offshore breeze kicked in for the more advanced sailors to perfect their techniques. Some experts even headed beyond the protective reef into the wave zone "to catch some air." We sat on the beach watching in awe.

Afternoons, we strolled to "downtown" single file along dirt paths by the side of the road worn down by foot traffic. Main Street Cabarete was nearly three-quarters of a mile long, starting a little to the east of our hotel. We passed a *colmado* that displayed a flank of meat hanging from a hook—generously attended by flies—as well as ample bunches of bananas, mangoes, plantains, and huge avocados piled invitingly in wooden crates. There were two small huts where friendly Dominicans were selling handmade items. I bought a small duck carved from stone that felt like satin to the touch and a tiny turtle hand-painted in bright green whose head nodded when moved. We also passed a car parked by the side of the road where a young man had new sneakers and jeans displayed on top of the hood and trunk. I thought of those bags filled with such items in the plane. He flapped a pair of jeans in front of me. "*Muy bonita*," he said, "*muy cheapo*." It was hard to resist his sales pitch.

And of course there was Laporte's pizza restaurant, open on three sides, where we stopped for lunch. Having been warned about the lack of sanitation in food preparation, we had our fill of his pizza during that week. While waiting for our order, I noticed a frightening crow's nest of electrical wires that ran overhead from the corner of his stand. It split into sections and joined other wires that drooped across the street to what barely passed as an electric pole. From there, the wires looped from pole to pole in both directions up and down the street, some disappearing into windows barred with thin jail-like grills. Continuing our stroll, there was a mysterious smell of things cooking in what looked like an oil drum that had been cut in half and used as an outdoor stove. This typical Dominican ingenuity was awesome.

*   *   *

The fourth day, we decided that it was time to find *Mamita's* that had been touted in the *Boston Globe* article, for a really cheap home-cooked meal. We asked everyone we met, *"Dónde está Mamita's?"* At the easternmost end of downtown Cabarete, a woman sitting in a rocker on the front porch of her house, waved us over. She pointed to herself: *Mamita,* and then to her mouth, and said: *comida?* in a questioning tone. The minute we nodded, *si, si,* she yelled to her kids to bring out three *mas sillas,* and seated us on the porch. One girl went into the house again, returning shortly with four glasses of water, which we discreetly avoided. We heard Mamita say something in rapid Spanish to a boy who was about sixteen and shooed him to the back of the house where I assumed that the cooking was done outdoors.

Then, we waited. And waited. And waited, not sure what was going on. (Later, we realized she had sent her son out to catch fish for our meal). *Mamita* finally beckoned us to join her entire family at the table in the house where she presented two fish on a platter cooked in their entirety: head, bones, scales, and guts— burnt to a T. At home, I only eat fish that doesn't smell or taste like fish, so I knew I was in trouble. She also served other biological forms of things I couldn't identify. Bill has often accused me of having a pampered palette, and now, I had to agree with him. I didn't want to be rude, but . . . you can imagine my distress. Looking in despair around the table, I saw one of the kids throw scraps to a dog waiting patiently. Dominican dogs seem to have the ability to eat and digest fish bones and whatever they can get hold of, since their owners don't have Purina on the shopping list. Then, still sitting inside *Mamita's* 100-degree house, I felt a very skinny cat weaving around my legs. Thus, piece by piece, I flipped some of the contents of my plate to the dog and the rest to the cat. We were all, the cat, the dog, and I, grateful for that arrangement.

* * *

On Wednesday, Bill needed to make a mid-week call to the office, and since there was no telephone service in Cabarete, we were advised to hail a bus for a ride to the nearby town of Sosúa, the one that we had passed on our way to Cabarete, where we would find a telephone booth . . . somewhere. The bus, called a *guagua*, which is derived from *Taino* (the indigenous Indian language) for transportation, was a ten-seater van that traveled back and forth between the airport in Puerto Plata and Cabarete and beyond. So we waited beside the busy street and soon heard loud Reggae music that preceded a beat-up van at least fifteen years old, packed with people. A man leaned out of the open door signaling us to get in. It was full, so we waved them by. Another *guagua* stopped—same vintage, equally as full—this time the young man leaned out of the doorway and grabbed my arm, pulling me inside. He did the same with Bill, Ann, and John. All the passengers were smiling encouragingly at us. After a quick count, Bill whispered that there were twenty-four people crammed into the van including us. I managed to perch one cheek on the edge of a board that was an extension of a seat, and when I turned to look for Ann, I was face to face with a baby goat, sitting on a woman's lap. I tried not to think about claustrophobia. Frightening speed got us to Sosúa in ten minutes, even though we had stopped to squeeze in one more passenger.

Downtown Sosúa was located on another crescent-shaped bay where vendors, taxi drivers, guides, and shoeshine boys were all on a mission to make tourists happy. It seemed a metropolis compared to Cabarete. While wandering around looking for the phone booth, we stopped by a plaza with park benches and monuments that were umbrellaed by an ancient, gigantic *Guanda Caste* tree which we were told was over 100 years old. We concluded that it was a popular meeting place for men, most of whom were smoking, gathered in the hot afternoon in pressed shirts and pants to play dominoes . . . with gusto! I listened to their melding voices arguing about baseball, the different rhythms of their speech, and their laughter as they slapped the dominoes loudly on the table with every play.

Talking to some of the shopkeepers, we discovered that many foreigners who originally came for a beach holiday had either stayed on or returned to establish their own expatriate communities—Germans, French, Austrians, Canadians and Americans who now lived in the DR year round. "We gathered barnacles down here," one expat explained, "we're just beach bums who came for the sun and the rum and were too stupefied to go back home." His comments sounded to me like a story he enjoyed and had repeated many times before.

It was fun stopping by the little open stalls with handmade items for sale, breathing in the intoxicating mix of exhaust fumes and Frangipani trees, and having lunch at PJ's where the walls were decorated with hundreds of license plates from the US. They offered up a lot of greasy fried food. But oh, so delicious. And always accompanied by a cold *Presidente*, the Dominican beer better known as *cerveza*. I've never cared for beer, but in the DR it was the safest thing to drink, which would buzz me into an afternoon siesta every time I imbibed. Due to a painfully memorable teenage rum and coke episode, I had no intention of trying the very popular Dominican rum by Brugal, the *other* national drink, unless it was disguised in a piña colada.

*   *   *

The city of Sosúa, located on a rise above the ocean on the east rim of Sosúa Bay, had a sheltered cove about a half-mile wide with a backdrop of towering cliffs joined to the sky by fragments of dark woodland. The water was calm and a deep shade of turquoise. One main attraction of the bay was the forty or more vendors that had set up shops right along the beach. All were hawking with exuberance. Signs everywhere boasted the best price. One even said, in English: *100% Discount.*

We learned that experienced divers could search for relics on sunken shipwrecks and coral reefs right there in the bay—and that there were underwater caves along the volcanic walls that rose up to the city beyond the short, sandy beach. The water didn't look at all appealing to me, and the beach couldn't hold a candle to Cabarete's.

*　*　*

On the fifth day of our vacation, we were soaking up some late-day sun. Ann, who preferred to walk way down the beach and sunbathe in seclusion, confided in me upon her return that she had two proposals of marriage by a couple of handsome Dominican men. Laughing, she concluded that they probably were looking for a free ride to the US, but I assured her it was really because she was such a babe.

John, our acknowledged reconnaissance man, jumped to his feet and announced that he was going for a walk. We had just been discussing what fun it would be to own a place of our own in Cabarete.

"Hey, John," I called after him, "if you can find a little house for sale, so we can each put up no more than five thousand bucks, then come back for us." We all laughed.

Less than forty minutes later, we saw John running down the beach toward us, waving his arms. "Come on, you guys, follow me," he said, "I found it!"

We dutifully followed him eastward, about a half mile up the road beyond the center of Cabarete where John led us to a tiny native house made of cinderblocks with a corrugated asbestos roof, directly across the street from the ocean. *Se Vende* was hand-painted on a sign next to the open door. Since no one was there, we decided to explore the inside. It was certainly primitive, but appeared to have a "working" bathroom, a kitchen with a stone sink that drained out to a drywell in the back yard, a living room, and one bedroom—about 600 square feet in all. BUT—*it had so much potential.* Bill, our engineer and builder, immediately paced off the lot as about thirty feet by eighty feet. The house was twenty by thirty.

It took the rest of our vacation to find the real-estate broker, dicker about the price, and agree to buy the little house for twenty thousand US dollars . . . five thousand dollars each, just as I had said to John. I realized then that in the future I had to watch what I said to him.

The *abogado's* office was on the second floor of an old stone building in Puerto Plata. He was a short, slim man with a pencil mustache and a nervous smile who spoke somewhat acceptable English, which was a relief to us. His one-room office was cluttered with piles of folders and plants that needed watering. We sat in the sweltering heat while he shuffled papers, finally producing one for us to sign. It was entirely in Spanish! Perhaps our enthusiasm had gotten ahead of common sense, but he seemed sincere, and we had invested in properties before, so we filled in our names and wrote checks. After *mucho* handshaking, Ann, John, Bill, and I bounded down the stairs with a rusty key in hand, hailed a *guagua*, and went directly to PJ's in Sosúa for a celebration *Presidente*.

Hopping another *guagua,* like pros now, we returned to Cabarete, disembarking directly in front of our new abode. We had the key but the door was open anyway. Excitedly, we moved through the house and around the outside, each probably taking mental note of what needed to be done. I'm not sure what the others were thinking, but I was picturing us planting banana trees and all kinds of Dominican flora and fauna around the tiny plot of land. Because the little house had once been painted white, we discussed calling it Casa Blanca, but then, thought better of it, being white North Americans in a Spanish country. So we settled on *Casa Cabarete.*

Our Dominican neighbors, Roque and Machita, were watching us somewhat suspiciously from the house next-door, until, through much gesticulation and terrible Spanish on my part, we informed them that we had just bought the house. Roque, who was dressed in camouflage pants and shirt, pointed with nicotine stained fingers, first at his eye and then at our house, and said: "*No problema.*" We interpreted his gesture to mean that he would keep an eye on our Casa Cabarete while we were gone. We all had big smiles and shook hands, agreeing that $20 per month would be generous for this service (about seven pesos to the dollar at that time). We shelled out six months' worth, 840 pesos, promising to pay the balance upon our return. Our newfound friend, our *watchy-man*, grinned like he had just won the lottery.

*   *   *

The ink on the sales agreement was probably still drying later that same afternoon as our plane took off from the Puerto Plata Airport, carrying us back to Boston with visions of returning the following February. Our long-term plan was to fix up our charming little dream house in the DR, and then after retiring in our late 60's . . . that's where we would live out our days.

All in one short but oh so wonderful week's vacation, we were in love with the Dominican Republic, and could hardly wait to return to our very own Casa Cabarete. Our retreat in the sun.

Main Street, Cabarete - 1998

DOS

1988 - FURNISHING CASA CABARETE

Back in New England, Cabarete was ever in my thoughts. Somewhere in my memory bank I recalled that Betty, a friend I had taught school with years before in Newton, had a cousin named Barbara who lived in the DR, and that Betty had visited her there on several occasions. Thinking about how to gather more intimate information about the DR, I called Betty who almost jumped through the phone with excitement when I told her that we had bought a house in Cabarete. She recited her cousin's address and phone number which, much to my surprise and delight was in downtown Puerto Plata.

During that ensuing year, in anticipation of our next vacation in the DR, Ann and I phoned back and forth declaring our findings and the bargain prices paid as we accumulated all kinds of household items for Casa Cabarete—pots, pans, linens, dishes, and silverware—some from yard sales, but mostly Goodwill stores for me, and Salvation Army outlets for Ann. We each packed them securely into strong banana boxes and stored them in our basements.

* * *

At last, February 1988. We arrived at Logan Airport with our boxes plus suitcases ready for our next Cabarete adventure. At the check-in, we were informed in no uncertain terms that no cardboard boxes were allowed on the plane. Cockroaches had a way of hiding in the corrugations, they explained. So we ran to a shop in the airport, paid an exorbitant price for two fancy oversized canvas bags with 36 inch long zippers; and right there in the middle of other passengers milling around, we transferred all our second-hand crap into those bags that had cost us about the same as if we had purchased everything new in the DR. Oh well, at that point, we were committed. After checking our suitcases and new duffel bags, we were finally at the boarding gate.

I was still used to dressing up for travel as I had in the 1970's, so halfway through the trip, while I peeled off my stockings and half-slip and dug in a bag for my sandals, everyone else was slipping into shorts, flip-flops, halters, and t-shirts in preparation for the blast of island heat that hits you just as you exit the plane.

And of course, we clapped enthusiastically upon landing.

I was excited because Betty had called the week before we left to let me know that her cousin Barbara had just sold her condo and would be moving into a completely furnished house right there in Puerto Plata, and further, Barbara wondered if we were interested in some of her furniture. Talk about synchronicity.

Being practical, we decided to spend our first night in Puerto Plata and meet with Barbara the next morning. John had located a hotel to which we could go directly from the airport. We arrived by cab at Barbara's condo at eight the next morning to introduce ourselves to her and take a look at what she wanted to sell. She was delightful to talk with us about the city and her life there. Without hesitation, we bought nearly everything she offered: two beds, night tables, dressers, a kitchen table and chairs, lamps, and a three piece set of pipe furniture with orange and yellow flowered print from her deck. We couldn't believe our luck, thanked her, and told her we'd be back with a truck.

Well, I can tell you, there was no such thing as a U-Haul in Puerto Plata, so in desperation, we rented the only truck available—a 20-foot open flatbed. Upon returning to Barbara's, she took one look at what we had rented, shook her head and hid in the apartment while Bill and John loaded and tied down all our purchases on the bed of the truck. One further drawback was that it only had a front seat. After trying to squeeze us all into the cab along with several pillows, Ann and I decided it would be far more comfortable to sit on the couch that Bill had anchored securely against the back of the cab. We held on for dear life as the load swayed slightly from side to side while we traveled the road whose conditions became increasingly worse as we neared Cabarete. What a sight we must have been—crazy *gringos* sitting out in the open with hair whipping around as Bill wove down the road reacting to the continuous directions of his co-pilot John who cautioned about potholes, pedestrians, goats, and children playing along the edge of the road. I think we girls were alternately screaming and laughing the entire trip. We continued through the center of Cabarete, observed I imagine, by curious tourists and amused natives as those *loco Americanos.*

*   *   *

Our house was just as we had remembered it although with an
eye to the load on the truck, it may have shrunk somewhat during
our absence. Nonetheless, we rolled up our sleeves. Ann and I
tackled the kitchen area, Bill and John offloaded the furniture.
Roque saluted us from his back yard and Machita brought over
some freshly cut pineapple.

What fun we had with those instant furnishings—one bed in
the only bedroom and since the second bed took up the entire
living room, we settled the porch furniture at one end of the
kitchen just behind the table and chairs. Next, we unpacked the
new zippered bags filled with all the items we had accumulated
over the past year. By late afternoon, with some tepid *Presidents,*
we flopped into a rocker and three wooden chairs which we had
placed on the front porch, just as a cooling breeze came out of the
east off the ocean. We were settled in, and it all felt cozy and
wonderful. I saw a goat tethered across the street nibbling on the
leaves of a flowering bush. His owner came by for him around
5:30. He walked down the road tapping the goat occasionally with
a piece of sugar cane. Going home.

Finally relaxed, we noticed the old two-part electrical wire
held up by rusty nails and draped through the rafters. It snaked
in from the front of the house, across the ceiling to the kitchen

where there was *one* bare 40-watt light bulb hanging from above. Checking for the connection to the outside pole, we saw clearly that the wires had bypassed the meter. Actually, Bill laughed when he observed that the wire went in the back of the empty meter casing and right on out the front. *Someone* had climbed the pole and spliced the house wire directly into the incredibly tangled mass of wires looping down from the pole. Fortunately, Ann had thought to bring candles and I, a flashlight. We soon discovered that the power company only delivered electricity to the Cabarete grid about six hours each day. The refrigerator that came with the house didn't do us much good. They say ignorance is bliss and I guess that's why nothing seemed to bother us. The boys decided that they would tackle the electricity problem *mañana*.

One *small* architectural detail of our *casa* that we hadn't paid attention to when buying the house last winter was that the interior walls sectioning off the bedroom from the bathroom from the living room were only about seven feet high, which left the whole house wide open up to the roof. Completely exhausted from the day, we were all tucked into our respective beds for the night, when John, who had a touch of Montezuma's revenge, got up to use the bathroom. Being a modest man, he tried to keep the sounds to a minimum. Finally, to relieve the situation, I yelled: "Let it rip, John." He did, and all four of us literally laughed ourselves silly. Some kind of ineffable connection between us always provided this kind of camaraderie.

*   *   *

Having paid for 24 hour use of the truck, we decided the next morning to do a little sightseeing before returning it to Puerto Plata. This time, we crammed into the cab together, knees and arms all intertwined, and bounced down the road, Bill behind the wheel trying to get a feel for our surroundings and John pointing out what parts of the road to avoid. After about ten miles heading east, we saw a sign for a beach resort with an attractively landscaped entranceway and decided to check it out. As we followed the road for a quarter of a mile lined with palm trees, the multiple plantings became more and more sparse, and then suddenly, there weren't any. And there wasn't any resort, either. Apparently, it had been a dream that ran out of money, but the broad empty beach was glorious and we had it completely to ourselves. Along the edge of the beach, there was a dark green, tough-looking shrub called Sea Grape, twisted and stunted, but thriving in the inhospitable terrain of sand and salt water. Some grew tall enough to provide a welcome shade. I tasted a grape and immediately spit it out. It was horribly sour. I pictured my mother who would have gathered them up and made them into jelly.

Striping to our underwear, we frolicked in the waves. From the water, I noticed a stray dog sniffing around our clothes, which we had left on a log. He appeared too curious, and so I raced out of the ocean to shoo him away. But, I was too late. For some crazy reason, he had actually pooped INTO my purse. Dead center! I was horrified and screamed as Bill, my Good Samaritan took over. He emptied my purse and then washed all its contents in the salt water. I know my companions were splitting their sides behind my back. I wanted to yell at that dog, but he had scurried away with his tail tucked between his legs.

When we returned toward the main road via the landscaped road-to-nowhere, Ann and I asked Bill to stop. We had decided to "selectively" choose a few of the plantings for the back yard of our new house. While we were harvesting, Bill suddenly drove off without us, obviously strongly disagreeing with our caper. We continued the harvest as Bill and John apparently had second thoughts, relented, and returned for us. Our punishment, perhaps, was that Ann and I had to ride on the open bed again in order to keep the plants from falling off.

By nightfall, Casa Cabarete had a much improved looking yard.

*   *   *

On the way back, I had observed children by the side of the road entertaining themselves with the simplest things: an old wheel from a bicycle, a stick, or a tin can, and every few miles, there were *colmados* where Dominicans purchased just what was needed for the day, since few houses had refrigeration. There were also rickety roadside snack stands where a friendly Dominican vendor would readily peel an orange for us or top a coconut with his machete.

Bill suddenly pulled to the side of the road, pointing out the window at probably an acre filled with orchids in shades of pink and fuchsia. To think . . . such beauty and no scent. I had never imagined seeing so many of those rare delicate flowers in one place.

*   *   *

We had not yet received the *título* to Casa Cabarete, so the first thing we did Monday morning was to contact the realtor that sold it to us only to find that she had returned to Idaho shortly after the sale. The grapevine revealed that she had been pregnant and went back home for proper medical care since the DR doctors are all too quick to perform C-sections. Perhaps not surprisingly, no one in her office could find our file.

We decided the next best approach was to revisit the *abogado* who had handled the closing. This required a trip to Puerto Plata, and upon arriving at his office we discovered that he had suddenly lost his ability to speak English. Through elaborate protestations of *no problema* and great hand waving, he gave us an address and some paperwork, directing us to the Land Registry Office where we stood in line for twenty minutes. They told us that the *título* was being held up—*we think that was what they were saying*—because we owed money for "tax stamps." Not totally sure, but relieved that there seemed to be a simple explanation and reasonable solution, we opened our wallets and paid generously—about five hundred US dollars. The man behind the counter then affixed numerous, very official looking, elaborately adorned gold stamps to an important looking paper, which he then handed to us with a reassuring grin.

At last, we had in hand our long overdue *título*. Or so we thought...

Returning to Cabarete by *guagua*, we stopped at PJ's in Sosúa for a celebration *Presidente* or two, and then back home for a dip in the ocean and a well-deserved *siesta* as official homeowners.

*   *   *

Like all vacations, the rest of ours passed in a blur. We spent our days reading, windsurfing (in the morning), beaching, playing cards, and acting domestic in our cozy little get-away in the islands. Bill and John fussed a bit with the plumbing and electrical items, but with our minimal needs—bottled water, store-bought ice, and a working toilet—we were satisfied. Roque and Machita were friendly and helpful; although I'm sure we must have seemed *muy estúpido* at times when we didn't have a clue to what they were telling us, even though we nodded our heads as though we did.

As we were returning home from Sosúa one day, the *guagua* stopped just west of Cabarete to let a few people out and a few more in. The stop was long enough for us to observe a construction project that was under way. It appeared that the workers were trying to erect a large, perhaps twenty-foot long pole that was to become the main supporting column for a circular roof . . . somewhat like a center tent pole. It was apparent that they were having extreme difficulty.

Just as our *guagua* started to pull away, I saw the pole fall to the ground and knew that Engineer Bill couldn't bear *not* offering his know-how. He nudged John, who had also been watching. "Come on Johnny. Let's give them a hand." They yelled for another quick stop and we all climbed out.

The three discouraged workers looked at us cautiously when *Gringo* Bill indicated that they would like to help. I love his quality of becoming involved in the moment. The problem, he knew, was not getting enough leverage to stand the pole up. Spotting two smaller, twelve-foot poles that were lying on the ground, Bill-the-engineer and John lashed them together to form a bipod about ten feet high. They then tied a rope around the center pole at the sixteen-foot mark and fed it over the bipod. Following Bill's actions and *directions-through-gesture*, the men got the bottom of the main pole snubbed into the center hole, and with the five of them spaced out along the length, they lifted it up. Easily. Cheers rang out from the guys and other on-lookers when the main column dropped vertically into place. *Muchas Gracias,* they said over and over, insisting on us joining them for a warm *cervesa*.

*   *   *

The few downtown shops in Cabarete and the characters that ran them were becoming more familiar. We noticed that gradually, we were acknowledged as word must have spread that we now "belonged" there. It was a good feeling. *Hang Ten*, one beach bar we frequented, offered a plate of spaghetti and a beer for $40 pesos RD (about $2.50 US). The added attraction in this place was an open area next to the tables with a Ping-Pong table where Ann and Bill competed furiously, usually punctuated by Ann's triumphant yelps. John and I were the cheering squad.

It was surprising that there were still so few Americans in Cabarete. Most tourists seemed to be French-Canadian or German, but typically, the menus were in four languages including Spanish and English. Although the waiters had probably not completed high school, they all were able to understand food orders given to them in any language.

Revisiting Auberge du Roy, we were surprised that the native village was gone from next door. In one short year, there were changes that had started to take place along the beach with the increase of tourism. Laporte told us that the Government had come in last fall and forcibly escorted all of the families, their animals, and their belongings to their "new" village located four miles out of Cabarete, across the highway from the ocean. The next day, bulldozers had leveled the village and huge controlled fires had consumed the rubble. In less than a week there was no trace of it. Bill commented to me that the process was like an eminent domain taking or Urban Renewal on a very large scale. I've always hated the idea of eminent domain . . . the intrusion of it, the feeling of powerlessness. Laporte said that the land along the oceanfront had been deemed too valuable for it not to be used for development into commercial projects. This was the first glimpse we had into the power of the Dominican government, now under President Balaguer. We read that Balaguer had ruled the DR people with a *sometimes* ruthless manner, reminiscent of his predecessor and patron, Trujillo, for six presidential terms which spanned the DR's arduous path from dictatorship to democracy.

But, surely there must have been a better way to increase tourism than to uproot these families who had lived by the ocean all their lives. I doubted if I could even imagine how they felt.

*   *   *

Over a *Presidente* at *Ono's Bar* on the beach, John suggested a one-day venture to round out our vacation. Mt. Isabella Del Torres was in Puerto Plata, he told us, 2,700 feet high with a great view of the ocean as well as the whole city of Puerto Plata below. We were game. Maybe we'd hike up next year, but for now, we decided to take a *guagua* right to the mountain, and ride up in the cable car, called *teleferico*.

The guide said that it accommodated about ten people, unless there was a crowd; then a few more—and there were no seats. The ride was quite a hair-raising experience as it swayed and chugged up the mountainside—a very steep incline. My knuckles turned white as I clutched a metal support beam, even as I observed the grand views of the old Puerto Plata bay in one direction, and lush palm tree-adorned mountainside in the other.

As we disembarked, and later when we waited on the loading platform for the *teleferico* to return us to terra firma, we were serenaded by a *Merengue* band that played enthusiastically. There was also an unusual guy, probably in his seventies, wearing a top hat, dreads, and sunglasses that started doing a funny little dance as he hopped around us, performing magic tricks with cards, coins, and foam balls. "Lookey, lookey," he kept saying to capture our attention . . . and a few pesos.

On top of Mt. Isabella, there was a bigger-than-life statue of Jesus Christ, similar to the one in Brazil. We walked the path through the boasted "botanical gardens" that were actually just flowerbeds in the shape of words, and dotted with tropical birds that I couldn't identify. After about 20 minutes of enjoying the view, I noticed that the wind had started to pick up and, beginning to feel anxious, I insisted that we take the return trip . . . NOW.

At first, my fellow travelers thought I was being annoying, but I noticed in their expressions something matching my terror when the *teleferico* swayed side to side at least ten feet from the centerline on the *very* silent trip down. Our descent was in February. In March, less than a month later, the *teleferico* was closed down "for safety reasons."

*   *   *

We had arranged with José, the taxi driver that had brought us to Cabarete from the airport, to pick us up at the end of our vacation. Most reluctantly, we loaded our suitcases into his cab and then went next door to say goodbye to our helpful neighbors.

Bill gave Roque our house key and the advance payment for his *watchy-man* labors, which he referred to as *feliz Navidad*. Once again, Roque pointed at his left eye and then at our house, assuring us that he would take good care of it.

Not knowing what to do with the trash that we had collected for the entire week in a large plastic bag, we had decided to find a dumpster on our way to the airport. But Roque reached into the taxi and pulled out the bag. *"No problema"* he told us confidently.

As José drove us away, I looked back to wave at Roque whom I saw twirl our bag of trash over his head and sling it into the dunes across the street from our house.

We consoled ourselves that hopefully, eventually, he was planning to burn it.

*   *   *

Back in New Hampshire, when Bill heard that a business associate of his was planning a vacation with another couple in March, he offered the use of Casa Cabarete, and they accepted. Hoping that Bill hadn't overstated the attributes of the house, I mailed a letter to Roque (in Spanish, ha-ha) telling him to expect visitors next door. Having labored over the letter, I *thought* I had arranged for him to "freshen" up the house in preparation for their arrival. At the time, we had no idea what a joke it was to have done that. Here's what our friends said happened:

The taxi let them out in front of the house. How quaint, they thought. It was about nine p.m. and very dark inside.

Fortunately, we had warned them to take along plenty of candles and a flashlight, which they used to briefly look around before preparing for bed. They had brought some basic foods with them that needed refrigeration. In the darkness, the refrigerator seemed to be full of something, but pushing whatever it was aside, they placed their items on a shelf.

Sometime during the night, there was loud insistent pounding on the back door that led to the kitchen. Our friend leaped out of bed, fumbled around for the flashlight and with heart pounding, walked through the kitchen to the back door where through the cracks he saw someone waving a machete. He shouted: *amigo de Señor Bill,* maybe six times before the man went away. Of course, it was Roque greeting our friends, but they didn't know that.

All four of our guests lay restless in their beds waiting for daybreak. Attempting to calm themselves in the morning, they decided to eat some of the food they had brought from home. Opening the refrigerator door, they found several pots full of meat of some kind and dead chickens, still with their feathers attached. Roque and Machita, we discovered later, did *not* have a large enough refrigerator, and saw no reason not to use ours.

Determined to overcome the drawbacks of this gifted *vacation* home, they muddled through that first day, checked out the beach and downtown and, judiciously, ate all meals in restaurants. Exhausted from lack of sleep, they did manage to make it through the second night.

Shortly after dawn, there was a horrendous blood-curdling screeching sound coming from the back yard next door. They all leapt out of bed, pulled on their clothes, and rushed out the back door. With trepidation, they peeked over the stone wall, and there, only a few feet away, was Roque right in the midst of slaughtering a pig. With blood still flowing from the slain animal strung by its hind legs from a rustic tripod, Roque gave them a broad tooth-gapped smile as he waved his machete at them. Horrified, they rushed back into the kitchen and stood there trembling.

Still attempting to make the best of it, as well as being exceptionally good sports, they walked to the center of Cabarete where they were able to charter a sailboat out of Sosúa, complete with a captain and lunch to be served on the high seas—and I do mean high seas. They were all seasick. Upon returning to Casa Cabarete, their friend's nausea turned into something worse; a flare up of his Crohn's disease.

Needless to say, they hastily packed up, locked the door behind them, and hailed a roaming taxi that dropped them off at the Auberge du Roy where they all contracted Montezuma's Revenge. I can only imagine the misery of waiting for their turn in the hallway bathroom.

Upon their grateful return to Massachusetts, both couples agreed they would never vacation in a developing country again. Ever.

We felt embarrassed and terribly regretful that their experience was so different from ours.

No Cardboard on the Plane

Mount Isabella Cable Car

Man with a Goat

Lifting the Center Pole

TRES

1989 - FIX AND REPAIR

For our third visit to the DR—this time for two weeks—the adventuresome foursome decided to fly to Santo Domingo, the capital of the DR located on the southern coast, and then travel by bus to Cabarete. This would give us the opportunity to see the country from another perspective. It would be about a five-hour ride on the bus, with a brief layover in Santiago.

Landing after dark, we took a cab directly to the hotel where we *thought* we had reservations. How foolish. The manager was most apologetic and directed us "just a few blocks away"—an easy walk—to a much more reasonable hotel where he was sure there would be rooms available. "Take a right at the end of our building, and you're almost there."

Feeling annoyed and exhausted—we had been traveling all day with a plane change in New York—we picked up our bags and left. One minute after turning the corner, there was only darkness. Across the way, a neon light that could have been the hotel beckoned to us. So we began to walk straight toward that sign, as the crow flies—on what seemed to be a path across an open field where we encountered burrs, mud, barbed wire, piles of ashes where garbage had been burned, and donkey plops. It felt like we trudged for miles.

We did gratefully check into the "el cheapo" hotel and slept like the dead. It's amazing how satisfied you can be with less than you thought you wanted.

Surveying the field in the morning, we saw that it was only a few hundred feet, but we had traversed it in the pitch black of night. All I could think was how lucky we had been not to have tripped or tangled in the barbed wire and needed medical attention.

Wandering around the thriving city, we observed telephones, politics, crime, charities, culture, museums, sophisticated people—and *truck rentals*. Worlds apart from the little fishing village on the north shore of the country that we came to know.

In a central plaza, there were plaques explaining how Santo Domingo had been a walled city, modeled after those of medieval Spain, and for three decades had been the seat of Spanish power and culture in the New World. No, I was not reading this in Spanish, there was a friendly young student who translated for us. He told us that today, the area known as the *Zona Colonial* stood as a monument to Spain's time as a superpower, with some of the buildings dating back to the early sixteenth century.

We walked through the city's old quarter which was a blend of colonial architecture, national monuments, cafés, bars, residential apartments, and *colmados*. But still, on the fringe of the city, life seemed more difficult and housing crowded, where fruits and vegetables usually there for the taking, as in Cabarete, did not grow by the side of the road. A country of haves and have-nots. Very little in-between.

*   *   *

The second night in Santo Domingo, we discovered an underground restaurant, *La Cava,* where the stone stairs descended steeply into a dark cave with candles perched on every nook and flat surface of the stonewalls. Mysterious and secret, the atmosphere was intriguing, even though we could hardly read the menu in the romantic candlelight. After cocktails, we settled on grouper, lightly grilled with *jicama* and potatoes wrapped in seaweed. Absolutely delicious. For dessert we ordered a decadent flaming dish, whose name I don't recall.

Finding ourselves anxious to get back to Cabarete, we departed the city a day sooner than planned, boarding a large bus with AC set so low that I had to draw the back of my full skirt up over my shoulders and huddle beneath it, still shivering. They served Dominican espresso coffee, this time sweetened and more palatable. We did stop for a bathroom call at a facility that I couldn't bring myself to use.

Santiago was a large modern city referred to as "the second capital". The streets were clean and people were bustling everywhere. A steady drizzle for the past thirty miles had slowed the bus' pace such that our layover was shortened to less than twenty minutes, so our plans to explore the city were canceled.

As in the outskirts of Cabarete, the rural village landscape along the way consisted of groupings of small rustic houses built of what appeared to be scrap boards and other miscellaneous materials, roofed over with rusty corrugated metal or asbestos sheets. Some had thatched roofs supported by palm tree posts or cement columns. Many of the homes were painted in bright pastels of peach, green, yellow, pink, and blue. During election times, we were told, house paint was generously donated in the villages by politicians so that the occupants could indicate support of his party by the color used. Rumor had it that if a house needed painting, and paint was offered, the party affiliation might be quickly altered. But then, that's probably true everywhere.

A feeling of tranquility came over me as we drove along; dogs lounged, goats and burros grazed peacefully by the side of the road, and the velvet-green quilt of the rolling hills in the distance drew my attention to a haze over the farthest mountain peaks. More and more, this Dominican world was becoming intriguing to me.

My stalwart companions slept peacefully next to me and across the aisle, while, being a people-watcher, I settled myself comfortably to observe a mini drama unfolding in the seats ahead. A tall, rugged, athletic-looking guy with a deep-water tan and a blond ponytail boarded the bus in Santiago and took the aisle seat directly in front of me. He wore old chinos and a faded blue shirt. Following closely behind him was a girl who looked about twenty-six, slim, wearing black socks rolled down to her ankles, a flowered skirt, and a white blouse. Her cheeks were flushed as she struggled with two bulging plastic bags. Her expression was sweet and her blue eyes twinkled through tiny rectangular glasses. She quickly slid into the vacant seat across the aisle from him.

I had the birds' eye seat and feigned reading my book.

The girl began by talking out loud to herself: "I can't believe I carried these bags all over Santiago," she said. "They're so heavy and then there was that Spanish kid who wanted my passport before he'd take my VISA card and I didn't understand what he was saying. I so want to hear *someone* speak English. Do you speak English by any chance?" she asked, now leaning across the aisle, smiling flirtatiously at the handsome fellow traveler.

"Yes, I do," he responded.

"Oh my God, that is so good to hear. You know, I've been looking everywhere for hair rinse the same color I use at home and at last I found it in Santiago. Can you believe it? But, anyway, I also had good luck finding a lovely dress to wear. I can use it at home, too. But I had to come all the way from Sosúa for these things. That's where I'm staying. Where are you staying?"

He turned slightly toward her. "In Sosúa."

"What a coincidence. You know, there's a disco there where you can dance until three a.m. I went Tuesday night and could hardly get up in the morning. We could go together if you want. I'll show you where it is. Oh, and here's a belt I got for myself," she said, pulling it out of a bag like a snake charmer. "It's a man's, but I met a neat cobbler-sort-of-guy in Sosúa, who I know would put some extra holes in it for me. It's great leather, don't you think? I might even go back and get ones for my father and brother." And without even taking a breath, she continued on: "What do you do?"

"I'm a solo sailor, going 'round the world."

"That's terrific. But you must get lonely," she said. "I'd love to go with you. If you come to Finland, you *must* stay with me. I have a little apartment with one bedroom but you could sleep on the couch if you want. I'd show you all around. It would be so much fun—we could go dancing. I love to travel. I always wanted to travel everywhere, like Africa and America, but I didn't have the money. Then there was this terrible accident . . . a fire . . . I lost everything, and the doctor told me to just take the insurance money and go. So here I am, my first trip, and to the Dominican Republic. I can hardly believe that we met each other. What kind of a boat do you travel in?"

"Well, right now I have a large Cat."

"This is too much. Can you believe it? I *love* cats. I had a cat, but lost her in the fire. I cried and cried. But I have a friend whose cat is going to have babies and she's promised me one when I get back. Maybe it could learn to ride on a boat. I'm so torn 'cause I work. You know, leaving it alone all day, but I think it will forgive me. Wow, we have a lot in common—you know, like dancing and cats."

The bus bumped to a stop and the driver called, "This is Altamira. Next stop, Sosúa." The sailor stood, and without a word or a backward glance, walked up the aisle and off the bus.

I watched as the girl from Finland pulled a flowered long-sleeved jacket that matched her skirt out of one of her bags. Arranging it around her shoulders, she hugged herself and leaning into the aisle, she looked back, directly at me. "The air conditioning is really too cold, don't you think?"

I couldn't have agreed more.

*   *   *

We were glad to depart the freezing bus at the station, which was on the west side of Sosúa. The heat of the day quickly caught up with us as we stuffed our bags into a taxi, eagerly anticipating getting settled in *Casa Cabarete*. The taxi delivered us *muy rápido* to our home. No sign of Roque or Machita when we unloaded the cab.

The key worked, but the door was badly swollen so Bill had to forcibly push it open. Once inside, the musty smell assailed us. The wooden louvers at the window openings were also stuck shut. Having arrived during a "blackout" time, it was hard to see clearly inside the house, but we forced the louvers open. Drawing straws as to which couple got which bedroom, we then dropped everything, jumped into our bathing suits, crossed the road, and climbed over the dune down to the beach to cool off in the welcoming tepid water. While we swam, the ocean breeze would air out the house.

Ann loved to float peacefully on her back, while I preferred to stand and watch the waves beyond the reef. Bill and John always swam way out, and then rode the foaming swells back to shore. Something magical . . . I looked down and there was a starfish, dragged from its mooring by the retreating water.

Since I don't like having salt water dry on my skin, I dibbed for the shower first when we returned to the house. The water gave one burst and then trickled to a stop. I stood there, soap in hand and yelled to Bill who informed me that there was no running water . . . no kidding, Sherlock. No electricity, no pump. When the lights went out, we learned quickly to say: *Se fue la luz* like everyone else in Cabarete.

And so began the rest of our vacation, soon to be named: F and R—every day: fix and repair.

Roque had a *moto concho* and willingly gave Bill and John rides for the many "fix-up" supplies to and from the *ferreteria*, about four miles east of our house. His willingness had been obtained by Bill who offered to run a water pipe and faucet from our well over to Roque's yard in exchange for the rides. One picture that sticks clearly in my mind was the two of them; Bill perched behind Roque, balancing three twenty-foot long *tubos* needed to repair our broken water pipes. They wove down the road with the pipes looking like the balance poles of a trapeze artist, blue smoke puffing out the stern of the motorbike.

The look of concentration on Bill's face was priceless.

A new water pump and rearranged piping from the shallow well finally brought a reasonable flow to the toilet, shower, and kitchen sink. Rogue suggested that a raised cistern would allow us to collect rainwater and store it at a level above the toilet, which meant we could flush and refill even if the pump was inoperative. That seemed like a great idea, and we contracted with a friend of his to build it right away. Only trouble was, the construction would take two weeks—long after we had gone home. We went ahead with it anyway, thinking of the following year.

* * *

One day, much to our surprise, a sudden rush of motorcycles roared past our house with *Hells Angels Quebec* printed across the back of the rider's jackets. We learned that even though they were reluctant to wear their colors in Quebec after close to 200 people had died in the bike gang's street wars in the 1980s; they wore them without fear in the DR, their adopted snowbird home. Impossible to miss, they were on the streets, in restaurants and even in bathing suits on the beach. As the first generation of Quebec Hells got older, the DR was apparently the ideal place to spend their golden years. The gang was thought to own hotels and a car rental company in Cabarete and Sosúa. At least, that's what the grapevine said.

* * *

While taking a relaxation break on our porch from the F and R, a young Dominican, maybe eighteen years old walked into our yard, introducing himself as *Lionel el pintor*. For clarity, he was moving his arm up and down as though stroking the house with a brush. He told us that he had a *bebé* and really needed to earn some *dinero*. Painting was one of the items on our lengthy list, so we decided to hire him to paint the corrugated asbestos roof as well as the house. Without allegiance to any political party, we chose all white paint.

Acting friendly as Dominicans do, he right away invited us to visit his home, which was a quarter mile east on the ocean side of the road. It turned out to be a tiny shack sitting on the edge of a dune that dropped off to the beach below with a magnificent view of Cabarete bay. Inside, the one small room was set up as a bedroom. The walls were painted turquoise; the floor seemed to be a hardened version of the earth outside. I didn't see a kitchen and assumed that they cooked outside. There was no apparent bathroom inside. Lionel introduced his wife who sat in their one chair and then proudly pointed out a poster of a famous baseball player. Lionel picked up his baby, holding her lovingly in his arms. He was so proud of his little family. We really liked his attitude, and felt good about hiring him. We advanced him *pesos* for the paint and the next morning he was on the job.

*   *   *

We had heard about Samaná, a city toward the east end of the country situated on a large bay. Humpback whales migrated there each year from the northern Atlantic Ocean to breed. It was over ninety miles from Cabarete and considered by Dominicans and visitors alike to be one of the prettiest parts of the island. Reminding ourselves that we were in fact on vacation, we decided to take a day off from "maintenance" to check it out and leased a car from the local rental shop, a short walk from the house. We learned later that all the cars at this shop belonged to various people in the neighborhood who wanted to pick up a few dollars now and then and that the rental "agent" took no responsibility for the reliability of the vehicle.

We left Casa Cabarete in the hands of Lionel-the-painter and the cistern builders and set out for Samaná with fingers crossed that the car would make it over the one and only highway, *Calle Principal*. Bill drove with John as co-pilot while Ann and I sat in the back of the beat-up '66 Chevy. The road was a mirage, liquid and rippling in the sun's glare.

Well, I can assure you that the trip seemed to never end—mile after mile in a car with no shocks, hardly capable of going more than 45 miles per hour, and even if it could, the rutted pot-holed road might have polished off the whole machine. On top of that, there was, of course, no air conditioning and the back windows would not go down. As we chugged along we ate the entire picnic that had been planned for some lush park in Samaná and I'm not sure how long afterwards that John fell asleep with the map on his lap, because we girls had already drifted off.

As Bill would later tell the story, after close to one and one-half hours of driving and no sign of Samaná . . . and no alert company within the car . . . he said to himself: *the hell with this*, and smoothly turned the car around without waking his passengers until he finally approached the outskirts of Cabarete. He then announced loudly, "Wake up. We're almost there." We three opened our eyes, stretched and peered out the windows as Casa Cabarete came into view.

It took a while to finally decide that the whole episode was, after all, pretty funny.

* * *

Before turning in the rental car, we decided to check out an all-you-can-eat buffet we had heard about at the *Tropicoco Restaurant* which was located on the west side of town, a little further than we wanted to walk, especially at night. Not quite sure where it was, Bill, Ann and I were on the lookout while John drove.

"There it is," Bill shouted. "Turn right here." And John, ever alert, quickly swung the car sharply to the right barely making it between two curbs that seemed to be an unusually narrow entrance. When the car straightened out, John hit the brakes just as the front wheels nudged the steps leading to the *Tropicoco* main dining room. Our headlights were pointed right into the eyes of the patrons at their tables. The owners, José and Ute, plus several waiters, raced toward us frantically waving and shouting: "*Alto, alto.*"

Apparently we had, with our small rental car, just fit through the sidewalk access for customers walking in from the street. You can imagine, with such a grand entrance why they never forgot us and always laughed when we showed up time and again for their mouth-watering international style buffet on Saturday nights.

When our daughter Julie B. and family came to visit, we of

course took them to *Tropicoco* where the grandchildren danced between courses to the music played by a lively Dominican trio while lanterns shimmered colorful hues across the floor. And for me, it was always a struggle *not* to start at the dessert buffet table for fear of not having enough room for the delectable creations. I always started with the strawberry short cake with oodles of real whipped cream, or the endless supply of Crème Brûlée.

One year, we went to *Tropicoco* for their Christmas Eve buffet. The tantalizing smells of what was to come greeted us as we entered. We passed along the buffet tables laden with fresh green salads and vegetables, and a platter of enticingly arranged mango, banana, avocado, papaya, and pineapple. Several chefs cooked while you waited: fish, pork, chicken and beef; my favorite was their red snapper cooked in coconut sauce. The entertainment that night turned out to be a Dominican re-enactment of The Three Kings. A parade of "actors" dressed as shepherds and kings with one child riding on a *live* donkey, wove its way between the fully occupied dining tables. This entourage was followed by another small child, smiling broadly, also dressed for the part, but carrying a dustpan and broom, ever ready in the event that the donkey forgot his manners.

*   *   *

Lounging on Cabarete beach a few days later, we were discussing what our next adventure would be, when Bill said, "How about climbing Pico Duarte?"

"Great idea," we three chorused. Having done a fair amount of mountain climbing in New Hampshire, and even though it was years ago when our kids were in grade school and junior high, we considered ourselves up for the challenge.

Later that afternoon John, fondly dubbed our tour director, appeared with a brochure in hand. "I have something I want to read to you," he announced.

*"Pico Duarte is the highest mountain in all of the Caribbean Islands (over **10,400** feet) with alpine forests near the top and rain forests on the way. It is named for Juan Pablo Duarte, one of the founding fathers of the Dominican Republic and is located in the central portion of the mountain range known as the Cordillera Central."*

"So, from Cabarete, we would have to bus to Santiago," Bill said.

"And then to Jaracaboa and La Ciénaga," John told us, "where the road is in very bad condition. I guess the landslides often close the road and we might have to get out and walk to avoid bottoming out the bus."

"Couldn't be worse than Cabarete roads," Bill said knowingly.

"All persons are required by the national park service to hire a local guide, and mules as well—you are not allowed to enter the park without one. The Valle de Tetero Route is strenuous, but is also more scenic. The Valle de Tetero itself is the most delightful part of the trek, with waterfalls, huge pools, and mountain meadows surrounded by trees full of colorful parrots and other birds."

The description sounded awesome and I was getting excited. John continued to read.

"Prepare for a pretty arduous trek. The first day in particular, climbing almost 4,400 feet over 11 miles from the trailhead in Ciénaga to La Compartición camp below the summit. Most inexperienced climbers find it pretty exhausting. Four to five days are recommended."

That was surprising. We had thought it would be a day trip, and I wasn't that sure about our endurance since I know Bill and I hadn't exactly been using a Stairmaster before arriving in the DR and I doubt if Ann and John had either.

"The mules can be ridden," John continued, *"and expect heavy rains (even in the dry season) and cold weather at any time. You may want to choose to pitch a tent because the cabins sometimes attract rats.*

"That does it," I screamed, thinking of my horror of rats. "Count me out."

It was a unanimous vote—we would pass on this adventure. Maybe the climbing of Pico Duarte would turn out to be like the trip down the *Gri-Gri*, a fresh water lagoon about one hour east of Cabarete, near Rió San Juan. It was advertised as an extraordinary ecosystem with a breathtaking view of crystal clear shimmering water and tropical birds and fish. Every visit to the DR we considered taking the *Gri-Gri* trip, and then for some reason, decided that we would definitely go the following year. Twenty years later, it's still on our list of things to do.

*   *   *

And then, another vacation in the DR came to an end. Although we had been discouraged about the condition of our little house, we always had good times together, as we did on this vacation in spite of having spent a large part of the two weeks repairing Casa Cabarete. Roque assured us once again that he would keep an eye on it for us, but this time, we weren't so sure.

As we sped down the runway and then lifted off, I watched the landscape opening up below, dominated by towering palms that were shadowed against the bright blue sky, where mountains reached the sea and everything was lush and green—a stark and tragic contrast with the denuded and barren landscape of neighboring Haiti.

Casa Cabarete

Lionel the Painter

CUARTRO

1990 - UNDAUNTED

Anticipation is a large part of any vacation, so on our fourth trip to the DR, we talked about the adventures we had had and those yet ahead. John, our designated travel agent flooded us with more pamphlets and ideas. Time and distance have a way of pandering to one's recall, allowing us to optimistically remember what we chose, and since we had left Casa Cabarete in pretty good shape, we were exuberant.

During the flight, we rehashed the improvements that had been made, along with plans for more that could be done. The guys even made sketches of a stairway that would lead up to a second-floor deck, high enough to see over the dune across the street (which, according to the realtor, could never be removed). At the right tide, the crashing waves on the reef that shot spray twenty to thirty feet into the air would be visible from the second floor. The new water pump we believed would be strong enough to supply a bathroom on the second floor as well, and the new cistern would ensure a reasonable supply of water. At least two bedrooms on the upper level were a must. In our minds, the addition was practically fait accompli. Or rather . . . *completo*.

You could not have found a happier, more eager foursome landing in Puerto Plata. We chatted away with the taxi driver, who may have had no idea of what we were saying, but he sure could tell that our spirits were high about something—only to be crushed the minute we arrived at the house.

The door was ajar. Not a good sign; as matter of fact, alarming. Bill and John rushed the twenty feet to the porch, peeked inside, and then signaled Ann and me to come take a look. Anticipating the worst, I quickly asked the taxi driver to wait before rushing to join them.

It only took a minute to realize that someone had been living in the house, or should I say, *using* it. Nothing was the way we had left it. Our furniture had been rearranged. The beds had been stripped of linens, the mattresses were stained. Beer bottles, filthy glasses, overflowing ashtrays—all were scattered around on the tables and floor. Our tour through the house was brief. Thank God no one was there as we wouldn't have known what to say, let alone what Bill and John might have done.

Out front again, shocked and crushed, we then noticed a sign in front of what had been Roque's house which made everything painfully clear:

DISCO – 10 pm to 4 am

Looking through Roque's open front door, we could see that the interior had been stripped to become a dance floor and bar. Without a word between us, we got back into the taxi and just sat there. Finally, I said, *"Vamos, por favor, señor."*

The driver grasped the situation immediately. Making a U-turn, he drove us back toward town. The first hotel we came to was about a half mile down the road, called the *Windsurf Apart Hotel*. I said, *"Pare aqui, por favor."* Feeling completely depressed and deflated, we paid the driver, and barely able to speak to each other, we booked two rooms.

*   *   *

While unpacking, I couldn't stop wondering how this could have happened. I felt angry and terribly sad. It was clear to me then that we had been enormously naive, even arrogant, to think that as Americans, we could just move into a native house surrounded by a totally unfamiliar culture and expect our intentions to be understood. We were the intruders, the two-weeks a year people spending money to decorate and play at life in the Caribbean, while all around us, Dominicans were eking out a survival existence. Unwittingly, we were "ugly Americans."

I tried to tell myself that we had been friendly and unassuming—and we had—not realizing that we were still miles apart from their reality. No matter how hard I tried to rethink our behavior, I could not come up with a plausible path back to living in Casa Cabarete. This realization was hard to accept.

Bill and I sat silently on the balcony of our room. The intense sun was caught in the limbs of a Frangipani tree that stood in full violet bloom right in the middle of the parking lot. Beauty such as that . . . it helped.

*   *   *

Still in shock, we gathered in the bar later that afternoon to sort out what had happened and to discuss with Ann and John where to go from there, let alone how to salvage our vacation. For me, Casa Cabarete was ruined and I had no desire to ever stay there again. I think that the feeling among us was mutual. Only time would help us accept the inevitable or contemplate what the future held for us in the DR.

Here is the story, as we later were able to put the facts together. Land ownership is a serious issue for Dominicans, and typically, the women have possession of the *título* as it passes to the oldest daughter. While some families may have built their homes and lived on the same land for years, they very possibly do not have legally registered ownership or title—even if they had paid someone for it.

Roque and Machita apparently had not owned the land their house was built upon and in which they had lived for fifteen years, so what happened was—their son-in-law, a Canadian, had conspired with the actual land owner and somehow forced them out of the house. He tore it apart, remodeled it into a disco which was open for business until four in the morning, playing ear-shattering music and . . . he used Casa Cabarete for "quickies" with his bevy of prostitutes.

There, I said it all in a couple of sentences.

Fate works in strange ways, as does the unspoken

communication between old friends. Somehow, a sense of acceptance evolved. Maybe each of the others had thought as I had about our unintended (or perhaps just naive) offenses, and had drawn the same conclusion.

That night, Bill spooned against my back as we lay in the unfamiliar bed. He cradled me with his powerful arms sending the message that we would be okay. With his reassurance flowing to me, I knew we would.

*   *   *

The Windsurf Apart Hotel was located on the eastern edge of town across the road from the ocean. It had an open reception area with a thatched roof offering an immediate Caribbean feeling of welcome. Catchy Merengue music was piped in from somewhere, accompanied by a colorful parrot prancing around in a large cage. He seemed to be looking at me, so I said, "Hi, how're you doing" and he said, "Wanna dance?"

There was a good-sized pool that was separated from the reception building by an outdoor bar that offered service on one side that opened to a dance floor, and on the other side, to people in the pool. We were told that live bands or talent shows were presented twice a week for guest activities, and there was an excursion desk where you could choose from all kinds of daytime adventures.

The three story high buildings going perpendicularly away from the road, facing west, consisted of one-bedroom apartments.

Paths lined by exotic flowering bushes, palm trees splayed with drooping combs, and low growing vermillion flowers wound through the yard and around the pool—the colors vibrant in the sunlight. Bill and I took apartment #312 on the third floor because it was farthest from the road noises and had a wonderful view of blue/black mountains in the distance, as well as a slice of ocean . . . if we leaned far enough out from the balcony. A small family-style restaurant served breakfast and lunch. Starting with each sunrise, tantalizing smells of fresh baked bread rose up from the kitchen, wafting into our apartment, and later in the day, the aroma of pizza cooking in the outdoor wood-fired grill.

* * *

We were determined not to waste the rest of our vacation lamenting the Casa Cabarete situation. After a four-way decision, we approached Borys, the booking clerk for the Windsurf Apart, and asked if he could possibly arrange for a full-time rental of Casa Cabarete. We thought that that could at least stop the current activities going on there until we could decide what to do with our abused little house. He agreed, and we wrote up a simple contract to make him our Casa Cabarete manager. We also asked him to oversee completion of the cistern and to deal with the outfall of the Disco next door. It was in his hands, for better or for worse, which allowed us to concentrate on vacation and fun as time was fleeting and moping about simply was not our style. Late afternoon, we found ourselves in the pool where two-for-one

Bahama Mamas were particularly delicious. We consumed them religiously while sitting in water up to our chests on the submerged barstools. It was there that we learned more about the Windsurf Apart from some of the "regular" guests. It had been owned and operated by Montreal-French Canadians reportedly connected with the mafia. Everyone apparently knew it, and no one seemed to care, including us.

*   *   *

Socorro, a lovely young Dominican woman who spoke perfect English, doubled as desk clerk and Windsurf Apart's knowledgeable and very efficient activities manager. So we were able to resume the original lure of Cabarete: Windsurfing. Socorro had an arrangement with the Bic Center, an operation on the beach that sold and rented all kinds of sailboards and ocean kayaks. We rented windsurf boards at a reduced rate, and continued to hone our skills. Bill by far was the star on that score.

My birthday seemed to fall during our vacations, and Ann never forgot. There was always a bouquet of flowers and a thoughtful surprise wrapped intriguingly and offered with love.

As official guests now, we could sign up for any activities. There was a day trip bus tour offered to a group going to Samaná Bay at the eastern end of the country—*"the hidden jewel in the Dominican Republic experience."* Of course, we already knew about the hidden jewel, but we were ready to really go there this time since Bill would not be driving.

Once in the city of Samaná, we would board a sailboat which looked like the Santa María. Then we'd cruise to Cayo Levantado, a small island created from a protruding coral reef which, we were told, protected Samaná bay from the Atlantic Ocean waves. Lunch would be served on the lovely beach flanked by tall coconut trees where we could snorkel among tropical fish and view the intricate coral formations.

Sounded great to me, and we signed up.

At 6:30 sharp on a slightly overcast Thursday morning the bus, which was mostly filled with vacationers from other hotels, picked us up along with a few others from the Windsurf Apart. We had with us, bathing suits, towels, sun lotion, bottled water. Snorkels, masks, fins, and vests were all provided by the folks who sponsored the trip. The cost included breakfast along the way.

About an hour into the two and a half hour trip, the bus stopped at a restaurant perched on the edge of the winding road that overlooked a verdant, lush vista across the valley to the distant mountains. Everyone piled out of the bus, converging at the buffet table laden with all kinds of Dominican dishes along with usual breakfast fare. I scooped onto my plate scrambled eggs, bacon, buttered toast, and a large helping of bite size mangos, piña, and papaya; then everyone to the bathroom, a brief stretch, and back on to the bus.

Not more than twenty minutes down the road I suddenly felt ill.

"I'm not doing too well," I told Bill who took one look at me and said, "You look like a ghost."

With that, I almost passed out. He draped me across a double seat and started to fan me with a snorkel fin. All I could do was curl up and moan. Ann and John, peering over the seat at me, decided that I had food poisoning. "It was either the bacon or the *refritos*," Bill added.

My head, my stomach, my whole body were alive, screaming at me. Bill held an empty potato chip bag up to my mouth. "Stick your finger down your throat," he suggested. I tried, but that didn't help. Neither did the nauseating smell of greasy chips. The only comforting thing to do was to moan and groan, which I did the rest of the ride stretched out in the back of the bus.

The guide wouldn't let me stay in the bus while the others took the sailboat to the island because it was going to be used for another job and wouldn't be back for our group until 4 pm. Bill and John literally carried me to the boat, and laid me out on the deck in the shade of the sail where I continued to moan, feeling even worse, if possible, from the gentle sway of the boat. When we reached the island, they again carried me to the shade of a palm tree. My *dear* husband and *dear* friends snorkeled, drank Piña Coladas, and swam in the turquoise waters while I thought I was dying.

Mid-afternoon, after what I heard later was a great luncheon spread, I was carried back onto the boat for the brief sail to the mainland dock; then guided onto the bus for the long ride back to Cabarete. By the time we got home, most of the nausea had passed and I was able to navigate, with a little help, to our room and most welcomed bed. Eventually, I did fall sound asleep. The next morning, in spite of hearing about the intriguing snorkeling, reluctantly, I forgave them for having so much fun without me.

*   *   *

I was fully recovered two days later when we joined Ann and John on their ground-floor balcony shortly after breakfast. It was another perfect day and our plan was to do a little more sightseeing. At the top of our list was the *Parque Nacionel La Isabela* where John's guidebook said Columbus had been buried. As we planned our trip, we saw and heard a drama unfolding in the apartment next door.

Two young men from the hotel housekeeping staff arrived at the adjacent deck carrying a queen size mattress between them and then disappeared inside the apartment, emerging after a few minutes with a different mattress. They leaned it against our railing, and immediately returned inside. A full ten minutes later, they staggered out with the gas stove, set it down for a better grip, and then took off with it down the path to the maintenance building behind the hotel.

A woman stalked out of the apartment onto her deck yelling at someone behind her: "This is a vacation from hell!" Obviously, she had not set her inner-disposition-clock to Caribbean time. Ann, being our social worker extraordinaire, stood up and reached her hand across the railing: "Hi, I'm Ann."

In no time flat, she learned that they were Karen and Roy from

Kansas City, and that they had exchanged a top-of-the-line timeshare week in Hawaii to come to Cabarete—much to their now obvious regret. Ann explained to us later that, hoping to turn things around for them, she asked if they would like to join us for the day. They jumped at the invitation.

We revised our rental car to a six-seated van and took off on our trip, a bit later than planned, but still in good time. The most direct route was to go through Puerto Plata to Lupéron, and then on to La Isabela, named after the queen of Spain in the time of Columbus.

While Bill navigated the always challenging roadways, John read to us from a brochure he had picked up at the Windsurf Apart's activity counter: *"The town of La Isabela was founded in 1494 on Columbus' second voyage and was considered the first European settlement in the new World. Seventeen ships carried and deposited 1,700 farmers, builders, and priests. Within two years, all but 300 had died of starvation and disease, and in 1498 the settlement was abandoned. Despite its brief existence, it is there that excavations revealed to historians and archaeologists that La Isabela was a substantial settlement with a church, public buildings, such as a customhouse and storehouse, private dwellings and an observation tower. It is also the only known settlement in the Americas where Columbus actually lived."*

Stopping for a late lunch at an open roadside restaurant that Socorro had recommended in Lupéron, we settled on squat wooden chairs around a wobbly plastic table. The lazy fan hanging from the ceiling stirring hopelessly at the air gave us little relief. Although we each found something on the menu to order, Karen sent back the first meal she chose and finally settled on chicken of some sort. While we ate, a couple of boys no more than ten years old started wiping the dust off our van and washing the windows, all the time looking over at us with charming smiles. Unable to resist those hopeful brown eyes, I offered them the large serving of French fries that came with my meal. They devoured them in no time at all. As we piled back into the van, Bill handed the boys some pesos. They ran alongside us for several hundred feet yelling: *Gracias, Americanos.*

La Isabela turned out to be a small town trying to exist on the meager tourist trade generated by the National Park. I considered it a tremendous disappointment. There was a barren, dusty park, probably close to one acre with little vegetation, and sectioned off with low fences that, according to each sign, showed where Columbus' house and a few other buildings had been. Baking in the afternoon sun was an open wooden coffin with a cloudy Plexiglas cover through which you could see human remains on view—reportedly to be Christopher Columbus himself. To me, they appeared in suspiciously good shape 500 years after having been interred. The museum building was more interesting, with displays illustrating the way the Taino natives lived, prepared food, and sustained themselves day-to-day.

Not long after looking around, siesta time beckoned to us four and since there were no other tourists around, we stretched out on the stone benches that were scattered around the park. Karen and Roy returned to the van, and waited. Patiently, I think.

Typical of DR weather in the afternoon, the sky suddenly clouded over and it started to rain. Quickly, we ran to the van, jumped in, and began the return trip. Barely under way, Roy passed a travel book that he must have been carrying with him up to John in the front, saying that he had thought we were going to see where Columbus was *really* buried, as was listed in his book. A few minutes later, John began to read from it: *"In 1992, a national symbol was constructed in Santo Domingo to mark the 500th anniversary of Christopher Columbus' arrival in the Americas, and is called the Faro de Colón, i.e. Columbus Lighthouse. Conceived by President Joaquín Balaguer when he was 85 years old and blind, it is an enormous concrete cross, flat on the ground, bursting with lights facing the sky. The physical remains of Columbus were moved from La Isabela to the lighthouse (although Spain and Cuba also claim to have them). Faro de Colón burns so brightly it can be seen from Puerto Rico, 150 miles to the east but, ironically, it is situated in the midst of a poor neighborhood where the people live without water or electricity and with unpaved streets and uncollected garbage. The celebration events were diminished by international criticism of the massive spending required to pay for this structure when millions of Ballaguer's countrymen were suffering from living in substandard conditions. A wall was built around the lighthouse to protect tourist from the neighborhood, and is protected by guards."*

At that point, it began to rain much harder. Once John's voice stopped, Roy commented from the back seat that he *knew* he had been right . . . that Columbus wasn't buried there. And then, no one spoke as the downpour increased. I was sitting behind Bill and could not even see the road. John tossed Roy's travel book on the floor and leaned forward, squinting through the windshield as the wipers went full speed. Daylight had faded and I felt like we were in the middle of nowhere. Bill was driving about twenty miles per hour, dodging potholes, with both hands gripping the wheel. When we finally made it back as far as Puerto Plata, the traffic really picked up. The rain became even more torrential. In spite of it, cars were actually trying to pass us, most with no taillights, forcing Bill to pull over so far that I thought we'd pitch into a culvert on top of a *moto concho* I saw lying on its side. Our van wallowed through huge puddles, slowing us further. We hit a deep dip in the road that was filled with water, and suddenly the lights and wipers became erratic, blinking threateningly.

It was at this point in the trip, when Bill threw the car in low gear and started whistling *"Dixie"* and John kept saying *"uh oh,"* that I knew we could be in trouble. I held my breath when the motor coughed, but somehow he coaxed it along, hugging the edge of the road. Ann was silent, gripping the edge of the seat. John kept announcing cautions: "hole on the left, drop off on the right, car heading straight at us, car stalled in the middle of taking a left turn . . ."

We came to a long uphill stretch when John hollered, "Construction on the right. Look out." And there was an open, water-filled trench, ready for a pipe installation ahead, right along the edge of the road. Bill clutched the wheel when a *moto concho* about fifty feet in front of us suddenly dropped into the ditch, such that only the upper half of the driver could be seen. As we passed him, he waved reassuringly, and yelled: *"total bien!"*

The rest of us had braced ourselves, absolutely rigid in the two back seats. Ann and I kept rolling our eyes at each other. I could only imagine what Karen and Roy were thinking. Bill whistled. John guided. We were three and a half hours into the two-hour trip home when I saw the sign for Cabarete. It was now near dark. Twenty minutes later, we pulled into the Windsurf Apart parking lot. Bill turned off the ignition and slumped down, resting his head on the steering wheel. The rest of us just sat there, except Karen and Roy, who without a word, opened the back door and made a dash for their apartment. We were glad to be back, not only because of the harrowing experience, but also because it was all-you-can-eat night at the Windsurf's *bofetada Dominica*. Quite unnerved by the excursion, but nonetheless famished, we agreed to meet in the dining room in twenty minutes.

* * *

Feeling refreshed after a hot shower and fresh clothes, we were greeted with a varied display of salads, pasta dishes, all kinds of fresh fruits and coconut, and *La Bandera*, (named "the flag" because the colors are the same as the Dominican flag). The popular national dish of white rice and red beans with stewed chicken and fried plantains, *La Bandera* is served in most homes and restaurants as a staple, the only variation is the meat . . . it could be chicken, beef, or pork. My preference would be without any meat at all, but that's not always an option.

After filling up at the buffet, we joined the crowd in the large open dining area where long tables had been set up next to the pool, fanning out around the dance area. There was a live band playing. A striking young woman who had been sitting at the end of our table suddenly jumped up and walked over to talk with the bandleader. A few minutes later, she was belting out *All by Myself* with passion and power. She really had a wonderful voice, which surprised us all.

I looked over at Ann who was talking with a good-looking Dominican man, a glass of scotch in front of her, and . . . she was puffing away on a cigarette! I turned to Bill and said, "Well, if Ann is going to smoke, I'm going to drink," and I promptly ordered a Brandy Alexander, my favorite when I do occasionally drink liquor—only on a full stomach—because it's made with milk and goes down like a coffee frappe. Thus reinforced, Bill and I jitterbugged like crazies, and after my second or third Alexander, we joined a tango line that wove all around the dance floor, the dinner tables, and the pool. The woman kept singing, calling for requests. When I yelled out: *Girl from Ipanema*, someone near me said, "That's a good one. She's Céline Dion's sister, you know." I thought she had sounded familiar, but had no idea that Céline's sister was a singer, too.

Drinks flowed and music blasted as we carried on after the buffet tables were cleared. Following my next Alexander, I felt like I was going to expire from the heat, and so—they say—I walked across the bar that spanned the end of the pool, threw off my dress and jumped in. Bill and Ann took one look, and with little hesitation, also jumped in, clothes and all. John then disappeared into his apartment and moments later came running out with a towel around his waist, dashed between the tables, leaped into the air, and just before he hit the water, whipped off the towel. He sunk out of sight, and then popped up with the towel wrapped like a turban around his head. The four of us were screaming, laughing, and romping in the water, when suddenly Karen appeared with a camera. About ten minutes later, Roy, in his bathrobe, called out from his deck for us to have a little consideration for those who wished to sleep.

More than a year later, totally out of context, Ann received a letter mailed to her address in Framingham. However, the note inside opened with: *Dear Jill and Bill*. It then went on to thank us for befriending them, and in hindsight, for helping them to have a "memorable" vacation. Enclosed were several blurry photos of us looking foolish in the Windsurf pool.

*   *   *

A day or so before our departure, we stopped by the front desk and Borys told us about his sister Ana and her three children who lived in Sabañeta de Yasica, a small coastal town fifteen minutes east of Cabarete. He said she would like to move into Casa Cabarete. We had visited Sabañeta two years before, looking for, of all things, flip-flops for me. It was more "commercial" than

Cabarete with a number of little shops that surprisingly had items not seen anywhere else, and at bargain prices. And yes, I found exactly what I wanted—ones that did not go between the toes. In fact, we had returned there before heading north to get another pair to take to New Hampshire. It was also the town where we had bought *tubos* and other construction supplies for Casa Cabarete.

Ana had been abandoned by her husband because she had contracted Bell's palsy and was now, in his opinion, "ugly." He was kicking her out of his family house (which he probably didn't even own according to our experience with Dominican home ownership laws). We wanted no involvement with those details, but I'm sure anyone could guess what we did . . . Ana and her children, Danny, Jimmy and their little sister, Viannely would be moving into Casa Cabarete as soon as the Disco mess was cleaned up. Borys thought the rent should be set at 100 pesos a month (about eight dollars US) since she didn't really have much, if any, income. Ana would take care of the property and pay for any utilities, of which, there were none.

While horribly disappointed that our dreams of retiring there later in life had been obliterated, we were relieved that this arrangement would at least help a Dominican family in real need.

Rocky's Night Club

John in the Pool

CINCO

1992 - IMMERSION

Taking a break in 1991, we enjoyed our winter vacation in Saint Lucia and then I spent March recovering from back surgery. But because memory has a way of softening certain events, we began to long for Cabarete—its beach sand, fine and soft as sugar, the afternoon vista filled with billowing sails darting across the bay— and of course, the wonderful people, romantic, loud, passionate, friendly. Hence, two years later, we found ourselves making arrangements to return to the DR.

John had called to advise us that we would be in Cabarete for the 500th Anniversary of Columbus' "discovery" of America, and that there were going to be parades and celebrations throughout the week. At first, I took the commemoration at face value until reading the following article in the DR News:

"The year 1992 marks the 500th anniversary, (El Quinto Centenario), of Christopher Columbus' opening of the Americas to European colonization. The Columbus Lighthouse (Faro de Colón), with an approximate cost of 400 million Dominican pesos, was erected, amidst great controversy, in honor of this occasion. Cristóbal Colón and Columbus Day are reviled in places because he is blamed for bringing the evils of slavery and the diseases of Europe to Latin America. He was avaricious, cruel and paved the

way for future conquerors (conquistas). As an example, Columbus and his cronies. . . "ordered all persons fourteen years or older to collect a certain quantity of gold every three months. When they brought it, they were given copper tokens to hang around their necks. Indians found without a copper token, had their hands cut off and bled to death.

Since the Caribbean had no gold, there were no copper tokens, but in Columbus' eyes, it had slavery aplenty. The Indians had been given an impossible task. The only gold around was bits of dust garnered from the streams. So they fled, were hunted down like dogs, and were either killed or forced into slavery.

Now, 500 plus years later, we recall his deeds and celebrate not Columbus the man, but the actions and influences of all the people who came after him, who melded their European culture with the indigenous cultures and, with difficulty, blood and years of battle, misunderstandings and treachery, have created the multi-cultural, multi-ethnic society we now celebrate with the Día de la Raza."

This certainly put a different slant on my perception of Columbus than as he is depicted in American history books.

*　*　*

Just as we climbed out of the taxi, a scooter past us puttering loudly, carrying an entire family; the young mother sitting side-saddle, holding a baby in her lap, her bright orange blouse rising above her waist, a young boy standing in front of his father, holding onto the handlebars, his hair wild in the wind of their movement.

Socorro gave us a wonderful greeting at the Windsurf Apart, as did Elizabeth who worked in housekeeping. We looked for Borys, our Casa Cabarete manager, only to find that he had left Cabarete for a position in Puerto Plata. So, one of the first things Bill wanted to do was to check out the Disco. I refused to go with him. He reported that it was not only shut down, but Roque's old house had been razed. However, Ana and children were firmly ensconced in Casa Cabarete.

Bill reported that the brightly colored couch and chairs we had left there were in the little parlor; a crucifix hung reassuringly on the wall over the bed. And in the kitchen, sunlight came through the louvered door leading to the back yard. Ana had kept the place clean and well cared for. Although she couldn't speak much English, she certainly recognized Bill and seemed most appreciative, he told me, to have been given the opportunity to live there.

Bill said that he felt better about Casa Cabarete, and satisfied for now to call the Windsurf Apart our DR home.

With the absence of Borys, we decided it was time to become acquainted with a reliable lawyer who would explain the intricacies of real estate laws in the DR—and, who could speak fluent English. An attorney in Sosúa who had acquired his education in the US was recommended, and we soon had a clear insight as to why we were never able to obtain a registered *título* for Casa Cabarete. Now we understood, but were not at all pleased.

Apparently, the woman from whom we bought the house had owned a large track of land in Cabarete from which over the years, small parcels had been divided off and sold. Each time, the number of sold acres was subtracted from the original plot total. Our tiny parcel, thirty feet by eighty feet, amounted to less than one tenth of an acre and was the last little section to be sold. Our original *abogado* apparently had "tried" to record our purchase, only to find out that there was no more land left on the owner's original deed. I'm sure this was no surprise to him; however, he refused to own up to it. It still rankles remembering that year when suddenly, no longer speaking any English at all, he had sent us to the registry for those fancy stamps and a whopping fee. It had been a hoax and a cover-up since we later found out he was a cousin to the property owner. The lawyer told us that there was no simple legal solution. Something Bill and I have learned through the years—lawyers do *not* like to sue each other.

It was infuriating, especially to Bill and me who thought of ourselves as fairly shrewd real estate investors. We felt stupid and naïve . . . somehow responsible for leading our friends astray, as well as ourselves.

Even though we were unable to solve the problem, we learned that one way to gain legitimacy in *título* would be to acquire a legal deed to an adjacent parcel, and then annex our little lot. Several possibilities came up, but by that time, the values had escalated beyond simple reach, and Ann and John thought it would be throwing good money after bad. We agreed.

The attorney advised us to just sit tight, be visible, active owners, and never admit to any *título* problem. He did say that we might not be able to ever sell the parcel without a clear *título*, but on the other hand, he doubted that anyone would be claiming ownership. This advice led us to extend Ana's lease indefinitely. As of this writing, she and her extended family still live in the house, these twenty-plus years later.

When we left this lawyer's office, the temperature had hit the mid-eighties; very low humidity. Scarlet-purple-pink bursts of color from a flowering bougainvillea vine scrambled up the walls of his building. I had seen the blossoms from the second floor window while we conferred with him. Watching for a *guagua*, we drifted down the street past a pink guesthouse with a ceiling fan whirring in its dim interior, then past an outdoor cafe with an enormous beer sign hanging next to a poster of a man who was running for mayor.

Accepting the sage advice of the lawyer, we began to feel more at home at the Windsurf Apart. There's something to be said for not having to be concerned with the daily Dominican challenges of plumbing issues, or electric outages . . . they had a generator. We could concentrate on immersing ourselves in the Dominican way of life. Not just getting to know the Windsurf personnel (and later, their families) like Elizabeth, Socorro, Jaime, Ramón, Alphonso, Felix, and Fernándo who always greeted us warmly, but also the resident population of Cabarete. While strolling around downtown, it was fun to recognize more and more people. We would smile, chat briefly, stumbling over Spanish phrases, and feel like we had gained another friend.

In Cabarete village, there was a *cambio*—moneychanger—a man who sat in a tiny, wooden, three-sided shack just big enough for himself and a table with a drawer that held his cash and a gun. The sign in front of his booth had Canada, US, Britain, German, and French exchange-to-pesos rates written in chalk so it could be updated at a moment's notice. We found that his rates were better than the banks in Sosuá or at the Windsurf Apart. After the first few times that we bought pesos from him, he recognized us and would call out, *amigo,* as we approached. We stopped more often after we learned that his rate was negotiable. Years after we started visiting the DR, the banks installed ATM's, but after a machine ate our card, twice, we either went *into* the bank or stuck with the guys on the street.

And then there were the lottery peddlers who walked around with a heavy wheel of tickets, holding out the end ticket toward every passerby, promising instant wealth to anyone who would listen. Everywhere you went, there he was with freshly laundered shirt and pants . . . I could hear his voice before he even came into view: "*Lotarial, ganar mucho dinero*".

*   *   *

While shopping for avocados and oranges from a roadside vendor, a handsome looking Haitian woman stopped me, took hold of my hair, and started to braid it. I pulled my head back and said, "No, no, *gracias.*" Not giving up easily, she showed me a handful of colorful plastic beads and tried again. *"Trenza,"* she said, *"muy bonita."* Bill suggested that if I tried the braids, it might help hide my frizzy hair that he heard about every time I looked in the mirror. I didn't go for it, although it was offered almost daily.

Everywhere we went, there were vendors on the street or cruising the beach. To them, it's their job, a way to help provide for their families. Washing car windows, selling homemade peanut brittle, hubcaps, jewelry, fresh fruit, T-shirts or pirated CDs—whatever they think someone will buy.

Our experience with shoeshine boys—*limpiabotas*—was on Cabarete beach. Generally, the Shiners live in *barrios* (slums) located on some of the back roads of Cabarete or behind the new construction of first-class hotels and upscale shops. A grievous contrast. There, families live in crude brightly painted houses with dirt floors, no electricity or running water . . . hard working families who fished and farmed, and sold whatever they could in order to survive. The Shiners build their own boxes out of scrap wood to provide a place to sit while working. There was a handle and a well for the supply of polishing rags and different kinds of polish. I could tell that the rate for a shine depended on whatever he thought you'd pay. They trolled the beach and around restaurants, where, while shining your shoes, their eyes were on your plate. Eyes that haunted me. I don't usually finish a meal, and so I would hand it over. Regardless of what it was, they'd woof it down and then pat their stomachs with a huge grin.

I always wondered . . . when was the last time they ate?

Maria, a dangerously tanned Canadian expat with whom we

were friendly, told us that these boys were forced to go out at an early age and that some Shiners were actually "pimped" by being forced to beg on the streets, and were usually left with only a few pesos of their take. Due to the competition that these *children* had to deal with, it had also become part of some Shiners' lives to act as drug dealers.

"It's because drug dealing is more profitable," she told us, "even though more dangerous. These kids, with no fear at all, walk up to potential customers and ask if they want any type of drugs. If a customer says yes, they scatter into the night and within minutes return with the drug of choice. If they are hassled by *policía,* they pay them off with whatever they are selling and continue on their way."

I didn't want to hear about the dark side of these boys. It was heartbreaking.

Once in Sosuá, we actually saw the *policía* chase a Shiner away because some tourists had complained that he was a nuisance. But, those kids didn't give up easily. Bill learned to only pay a Shiner in pesos, not American change, because the *cambio* places wouldn't accept it and the kids ended up with money that was useless to them. They didn't know the value of quarters and dimes. We were generous with tips especially after hearing Maria's description of their lives in the *barrios* from which most visitors are insulated.

Un día sin trabajo es un día sin comida. A day without work is a day without food.

*   *   *

Maria, who was a masseuse in high demand, had formerly run her business out of one of the Windsurf apartments. She regaled us with stories of the early days of Cabarete. She told us that she had managed John Laporte's first Pizza parlor. Her massage business was now in the center of town conveniently located in a second-story apartment overlooking the beach. Person after person spoke of the strength and magic of her hands, and how she had straightened out their misaligned backs.

While sitting on the beach with Maria one late afternoon, a man approached us, thrusting a bottle under our noses, saying "*mamajuana se vende.*" I glanced around nervously and then pushed his hand away, surprised that they would sell it so openly on the beach. Maria couldn't stop poking fun at my reaction. It seems that anywhere you travel in the world, each country has its own native drink, and in the DR, it is known as *mamajuana.*

At first glance, it looks like a wine bottle filled with a concoction of sticks, leaves, and roots, not something you'd want to drink. Marie told us that they "cure" the pieces of *guyacan* wood and *Canilillea* leaves by adding cheap gin (or red wine and honey—a matter of personal preference) and let it sit for six weeks to get the bitterness out. Then after pouring out the gin, which kills any harmful bacteria, dark rum is added to fill the remaining space, generally 40% to 90% proof. "For an extra kick," she said, "most guys like to add something stronger, like 151 proof rum." Undoubtedly, notwithstanding the combination of these ingredients, the rum was what provides *mamajuana* with its mythical status of having rare powers. Legend had it that it acted as somewhat of a cure-all for everything from *la gripe* (the Dominican term for the flu), to a variety of ailments ranging from prostate to ovarian disorders. However, *mamajuana* had gained specific notoriety among Dominicans for its rumored ability to increase vitality and act as an extremely powerful natural aphrodisiac. A homegrown version of today's Viagra. No wonder it was so popular. I bought a small bottle and grinned at Bill. After taking a long pull which made me gag, we left it sitting on the beach for any seasoned fan who wanted it.

*   *   *

La Casita, the tiny restaurant on the beach that everybody recommended, was most famous for its fresh *camarones* (shrimp) and langoustines (lobster). Papi, the owner, worked in an open kitchen where anyone could watch as he prepared his secret garlic cream sauce (probably with some kind of liquor added) that was served with the most tremendous platter of shrimp I have ever seen. He accepted reservations, so we stopped by in the morning to put our name in for 7pm. Even then, the sound of voices and clatter of saucepans coming from the kitchen was convincing, as well as the smell of something delicious.

When we arrived that evening, there were tables arranged on the beach in addition to a more intimate setup on the second floor over the kitchen, which became my favorite place to eat. They started us out with dainty seafood sandwiches and drinks of choice while we waited in the glow of strings of colorful lights and the murmur of two or three different languages from the surrounding tables.

And then . . . the pièce de résistance (pieza de resistencia?) ... Papi's *camarones* in cream sauce. To die for. They were still in the shells, so we worked at feeding ourselves. The juice ran down our arms, but we didn't care. The tide was out and the moon was bright, shimmering on the wet sand.

Along with the check that was placed in a conch shell, were a pile of napkins and a bowl of warm lemon water in which to wash. For our next visit to Papi's La Casita, Ann suggested that we order only two platters of *camarones*, and even then we'd have more than a gentle sufficiency.

The following night, we walked to a native restaurant located in the *barrio* just west of town. It had a *cana* roof but no walls, and the kitchen was in the back, out of sight. I always felt a bit nervous choosing what to order in a place like that, worrying about sanitation and contaminated water. Twenty-five watt bulbs didn't do much for reading the menu so I ordered *arros con pollo*, a fairly safe choice. They had just served us *Presidentes* and placed a basket of garlic toast on the table, when out of nowhere, a donkey stuck his head between the supporting columns and scoffed a piece of garlic bread that was sitting on my plate. I must have let out a loud yelp because the waiter ran out with a broom to chase him away. Upon his return, he shrugged apologetically and said, *"Mi amigo."*

Returning to our condo, Ann and I were walking ahead of the boys. I turned around to find out what was keeping them, and saw that they were talking to two *ladies of the night*. They both had glamorous hairstyles and wore staggeringly high heels, hot pink miniskirts, and tank tops they *almost* had on. One of the girls looked up as we approached. She turned to Bill and John and said: *"Sus esposas?"* When the guys (reluctantly? sheepishly?) nodded *Si,* she grabbed her friend's arm and they took off at a rapid pace. We laughed all the way back to the Windsurf. A sense of relief came over me then . . . realizing that we were able to move beyond our disappointment about Casa Cabarete and enjoy our vacation together.

The Christmas Donkey

Bill, John, Julie and Ann dining at the Windsurf 1992

Talia and Elan at La Casita

Sandra, Social Director at the Windsurf

SEIS

1996 - 1998 - WINDSURF RESORT

Perhaps it was the lingering disillusionment of our Casa Cabarete venture that caused the four of us to take different vacations over the next several years, visiting other places, some together, some with other friends. But eventually, the lure of Cabarete became too much for us to resist, and 1996 found us once again joining the exuberance as we landed in Puerto Plata.

We had also been urged to return to Cabarete by daughter Shary, while sitting on the deck at the Lakehouse in August, discussing what had happened with our Casa Cabarete. She opened a book by Henry David Thoreau and read this quote: *If we will be quiet and ready enough, we shall find compensation in every disappointment.*

Cabarete had grown immensely; it seems to hum from dawn to dusk. New hotels and restaurants lined the main street and the beach, where tourists in speedos and bikinis no matter age or body type, carrying floppy hats, towels, books, and sun lotion, rushed in early morning to claim a lounge chair, their skin already red from yesterday's sun. In my youth, I used a mixture of iodine and baby oil to enhance my tan—*horrors*—but have long since stopped worshipping the sun. Now I just shake my head at these eager beach goers.

*   *   *

John, with his usual curiosity, found out that the Windsurf Apart had been purchased in '95 by three Canadians from Winnipeg (referred to as Winnipeggers or just Peggers), and was renamed The Windsurf Resort. It had become a member of Interval International, a worldwide time-sharing company. It was then that we met Gordon, age 36, about the same as our son Stevie. Acting as the on-site partner in charge, he had a welcome smile and an 'aw shucks' demeanor. His two other partners/owners visited from Canada every now and then, but he was the lead man in the DR. You couldn't help but like his style and exuberance. His father, Hugh, an experienced Canadian builder, had already constructed two additional three-story buildings on the west side of the Windsurf pool, each consisting of six two-bedroom lockout type units. He was now helping with the day-to-day management of the newly named Windsurf Resort. The additions looked terrific, as did other improvements at the resort.

Socorro was working full time at the Reception Desk, while Sandra, a pretty Canadian gal who bebopped around town on her motor scooter, was the full time Social Director who gave brief orientation speeches on Wednesdays and Sundays—the days that new guests arrived—mostly from Canada and Europe. She added so much to the resort with her fun-loving personality and enthusiasm for Cabarete. Ann and I agreed that we loved the changes all around.

While lunching by the pool one day, we watched a man hang large artistic figures of native scenes made of pierced, hammered metal on the walls of the dining room. They were backlit, which produced an interesting silhouette effect. Hugh came by, gave the man thumbs up, and then proceeded to guide him to our table for an introduction.

"This is Doug. He's an eclectic artist in about any form you can imagine, including the kitchen," he told us four.

With that, he left, and Doug, a friendly guy probably in his early fifties, sat down and began to recount the funny story of how he became the chef at The Castle Club, a restaurant that he and his wife, Marguerite, ran out of their home. A few years before, they had received a phone call around noontime from a distraught neighbor who said that she had unexpected guests coming for an overnight visit—on the tail of other friends who had just left that morning—and that she was completely exhausted and could not imagine cooking another thing.

"Could I possibly entice you guys into inviting us and our new guests over for dinner?" Doug quoted her. "You prepare it, and of course we'll pay you for all the expenses."

"We said yes," Doug told us, throwing his hand up as though in surrender, "and that was the birth of our Castle Club. Our home could hardly be called a restaurant," he added, smiling broadly, "but rather, we think of it as an evening experience that includes fine gourmet cuisine provided by yours truly. We now promote The Castle Club as our business by soliciting small dinner parties through resorts and hotels."

It sounded so intriguing that as soon as he left, we raced to the front desk to make reservations for the soonest possible date. Socorro booked us that next Thursday with four other couples and told us it was a twenty-minute taxi ride from Cabarete. We arranged for the taxi with José. He knew all about the Castle Club routine and told us he would pick us up at the Windsurf at six, deliver us, and then return to take us home at nine. I could hardly wait.

On the appointed day, José drove us through Sabañeta, turning south on the road to Moca; it snaked up into the mountains. We could see a church steeple below and every few miles, a group of weather-beaten houses appeared in clusters, their roofs extended over bare earth with a few plastic chairs placed in the shade. There was the smell of something cooking. The air turned cooler.

I suddenly saw a small sign: *The Castle Club*, just as José took a sharp turn off the road onto a nearly impassable dirt driveway. The taxi bumped and swayed for another half mile. José stopped once to open a gate, and then he drove up a long, steep hill to the entrance of The Castle Club, with bougainvillea vines hanging from the doorway like purple mantles. We were greeted like old friends by our charming hosts who stood at the top of broad stone stairs in front of massive wooden double doors. Flanked by three black Dobermans, they invited us into their unique and wonderful home. Marguerite, Doug's wife, was lovely, gregarious, and a quintessential hostess, just as he had told us.

Surrounded on all sides by hills, open fields, and palm trees, The Castle Club sat atop a hill of its own, with extraordinary vistas of the mountains and palm-studded valley, where to the north, we were told, on a clear day, a faint glimmer of the ocean could be seen.

I don't know what I was expecting, but stepping inside we were greeted with a truly extraordinary home, completely open to the mountains along one wall, with a cathedral-ceilinged living room, approximately twenty-four feet wide by forty feet long with a large fireplace at one end. There were multiple arches, stone floors, artifacts, and unique artwork they had acquired over the years, in addition to numerous original pieces by Doug. In the two adjoining dining rooms, Marguerite had set the tables with candles and rose petals on antique lace tablecloths. There was a concrete circular stairway leading up to the yet-to-be-finished second floor, which would consist of three bedrooms and two baths, as soon as the chef/artist/metal worker—the multi-talented Doug—could get to it.

Doug and Marguerite, formerly from the United States, had originally hired a presumably reputable Dominican contractor, who, after building the initial structure on their magnificent setting, continued to request more and more funds from the absentee owners, and then ran off with most of it. As we had already discovered, the driveway was part of the unfinished job. Marguerite told us her wonderfully accomplished husband had been finishing the house—a labor of love and work in progress—

over the last five years, with still more to go.

During cocktail time with hors d'oeuvres of miniature pesto quiches filled with homemade goat cheese, we were free to explore the structure and spend time on the outdoor patio overlooking a vegetable garden and swimming pool, and a sunset that rivaled any place in the world. Wherever we went, we were accompanied by at least one of their Dobermans, who were friendly to guests, but apparently thoroughly discouraged any nighttime intruders. Following a mouth-watering aroma, Bill and I wandered into the gourmet kitchen with multi-colored Spanish tiles set on massive granite counters, and joined Ann and John who were chatting with other guests and our hosts while they prepared our dinner.

While wine flowed, the meal started with Caribbean carrot soup, followed by grouper with Doug's special lobster sauce, rice pilaf, and an organic salad of fresh greens from their garden. For dessert, Bill loved Marguerite's rum chocolate mousse— a chocoholic's dream.

José arrived for the return trip, as planned. It felt like we were saying thanks and goodnight to old friends. Descending from the hills and the enchantment of the evening, we came back to earth in the center of Sabañeta where we passed a gas station next to an open, crowded pavilion with blinking green lights. About twenty Dominicans were dancing to loud Merengue, while a lone guard sat tilted back against a gas pump in a wooden chair, a rifle rested across his lap as he bobbed his head to the music. Dominican law and order in process.

*   *   *

Each Friday night at the Windsurf, there was entertainment around the pool with music—very loud music—right below Unit No. 312, our original and now favorite third floor apartment. There was dancing and singing with a PA system that would rival any teenage boom box. We loved to watch the sheer showmanship and passion of Dominicans as they danced. Listening from our balcony, we heard, in English: "jitterbug contest." It took less than a minute for us to look at each other and decide to compete; tearing down the three flights of stairs, already out of breath, Bill and I joined the competitors, looking, I imagine, as though we thought we were still teenyboppers.

Benny Goodman, with whose band my father played violin in the 1920s, is credited with establishing the Swing Craze that had started the jitterbug. The best style depends on what type of music you are dancing to at the time, and, once on this Dominican dance floor, we were greeted with a combination of Merengue, Bachata, Salsa, and Reggaetón, to which there is no best way to swing. So we improvised with our own style of the Lindy—a frenetic, acrobatic, fast-dance. The floor was crowded with vacationers and Dominicans alike, the music got louder and louder and we began to think that the competition would never end. Ann and John were sitting this one out.

Guess what? We got first prize for American couples over 55. How *ever* did they guess our ages as we accepted our award panting and perspiring? Nonetheless, we proudly staggered back up the stairs, each with a T-shirt that said *Windsurf Resort* on the front, and a picture of a windsurfer on the back. Shrunken and faded, we still have those shirts today. As I think on it, maybe they didn't shrink. Maybe we just expanded.

*　　*　　*

Walking downtown for lunch one day, Bill and I suddenly found ourselves on a crowded sidewalk among enthusiastic Dominicans who were cheering the newly elected president, Leonel Fernández as he drove by in an open convertible, his political speech blaring from loudspeakers. He was part of the Dominican Liberation Party.

Having just defeated Balaguer who had served as president for 22 years, Leonel, sitting proudly in the center of his motorcade, brought hundreds of people to line the main street of Cabarete chanting: *.Leonel, Leonel . . .* while repeatedly raising their hands with index finger and thumb forming an **L.** We joined right in with the honorary salute, wanting to support his election.

The change in the political climate was palpable. We could feel it. Gone were the days of dictatorship, civil war, political unrest, the patriarch, although it was obvious that Leonel had a daunting task ahead to fight the old ways of government and the tradition of political patronage. But everyone we talked to was feeling optimistic for a brighter future.

*   *   *

Baseball is the sport the DR loves. I have seen boys everywhere—in the streets, on the beach, and in vacant lots—improvising with pieces of cardboard contoured over their hands as gloves, ragged baseballs, and broomsticks tied together for bats . . . any way they could emulate their baseball heroes who had achieved more success than they could even dream of.

When our daughter, Julie B. and family came to visit, our son-in-law, Ari, whose passion is baseball, told us that the Dominican-born Sammy Sosa had been a shoeshine boy who learned his baseball talents on Cabarete beach. And about Pedro Martinez who was a Red Sox player, "arguably the greatest pitcher of all time," Ari added with a look that suggested envy. We learned the sad story of Pedro's father who was a pitching phenomenon in the DR. He was invited to tryout with the San Francisco Giants but apparently he never showed up because he couldn't pull together enough money for a passport and airfare. He spent his life as a janitor, barely making enough money to support his six children.

One afternoon, Ari and our grandson, Elan, walked down the road, past Casa Cabarete, took a right on a dirt road that looked more like a cow path, and on another quarter mile to the "ball field" where chickens and dogs roamed about in the outfield. The field blended into the homes surrounding it. The people milling around the field were part spectators and part neighbors out to share time with friends.

Elan told us that the balls were tattered—barely recognizable as a baseball, and that there were no foul lines, no fences, and no discernible borders defining the field. The players bantered with the spectators during the game.

"We were not watching a game of baseball," Ari said. "We were watching life in the DR. Having coached Little League for several years, it was fun for me to see the fervor these kids had for the game. Baseball was not only an event neatly embedded into the sequence of their day, it was their reflection woven into the fabric of Dominican culture. It was amazing."

It was no surprise that on this vacation Ari took the family to Santiago where major leaguers were playing in the final series for the championship of the DR. The tickets cost $8 dollars. "Incredible," he had said, "compared to US prices." When they approached the field, he told us that he could hear the crack of bats as the hitters warmed up and the cheers of the crowd dissolved into the dark humid sky. He was really pleased at the casual family-friendly atmosphere. Players chatted with spectators, and signed programs for souvenirs. He was a little disappointed with the condition of the field for a big league: the grass full of large brown patches, but what could you expect with such low prices.

Ari's interest in baseball has been life-long, cumulating in pitching in the first year of the Israeli Baseball League. When I asked about the Santiago game, he said, "Pedro became a legend not only in the DR but also in Red Sox nation and in the entire world of baseball. And by the way," Ari added, "Pedro and I have something in common. We were both signed by previous Red Sox General Manager (currently the GM of the Orioles) Dan Duquette."

After the game, Julie B. told us about an ethnic, out-of-the-way restaurant they had found in a residential neighborhood just off the main square in Santiago—her favorite kind of place to eat. A woman had beckoned them to come into her small home where there were just a few tables and chairs set up. She spoke some English with a strong Italian accent. After figuring out something that they recognized on the menu and then ordering, the woman suddenly yanked the menus out of their hands. "No, no, not that," she said, "that's no good. I order for you."

According to Julie B, whatever she served them was super delicious. After dinner Ari asked the woman about the statue of a man he had noticed in the corner of the garden.

"That's Columbus, the son-of-a-bitch, he raped our people. He no good."

Of course the children wondered why she kept the statue in her garden, but didn't dare to ask. She and her daughter served the best meal they had had in the DR.

Returning to Cabarete, Elan told us that they passed a weird sight: "There were cages or crates along the highway piled three high and filled with birds. They were crammed in together just sitting there with no people around." When I asked if they were chickens, he wasn't sure.

Bill and I had it in mind to look for that restaurant they had mentioned the next time we went to Santiago.

*   *   *

While lounging by the pool a couple weeks later, Gordon stopped by to chat. He was working hard to sell the Windsurf units as timeshares. Before leaving that year, Ann and John bought one week, not only thinking about their kids, but about the exchange possibilities since they love to travel.

Gordon also spoke longingly of the large lot of land next to the hotel. "It's for sale at a giveaway price," he told us. He skipped a beat, gave us his charming look, and then said: "You aren't interested in investing, are you?"

After a significant look passed between Bill and me, I quipped right back: "No thanks. But we might be interested in *buying* instead of timesharing, unit No. 312. The one we're staying in now."

Boy, did his eyes light up. He said, "Cash?"

And I shot right back, "Depends on the price."

Realizing that we would not return to Casa Cabarete in the near future helped us to come to an agreement, so a purchase and sale contract was generated and signed all around. As part of the sale, we wanted some remodeling done to No. 312 before our return to the DR. Bill set-to, drawing up the modifications, as that is something he is so good at and loves to do.

Bill and I were thrilled at the thought of owning a unit that would be sitting there waiting for us whenever we chose to return. Ann and John thought we were nuts and maybe we were, but that was the way Bill and I operated—we jumped into one adventure after another, and with the exception of a few miscalculations, have been pleased with our enthusiastic decisions. Just before we left for New Hampshire, we caught Gordon in the lobby and asked if the título to No. 312 had come through, to which he replied with an assuring smile, *mañana*, an answer we have learned to expect. It meant—don't hold your breath while you're waiting.

Slowly, we were learning that there was no straightforward transaction in the DR. There could be two prices, one for Dominicans, one for tourists, whether it was over real estate or a handmade trinket for sale on the beach.

During the following summer we communicated with Gordon, wondering where the title was, so that the deed could be filed. Yes, here we were again with confusion about a Dominican *título*. What was going to be the story this time, I wondered. Well, it was a doozie.

When Gordon and partners had bought the Windsurf Apart from the Montreal group, they thought they were buying everything, including land, buildings, and *all* apartments. But, no. Apparently a few of the apartments had been sold individually and mysteriously, still belonged to someone else. We found out that No. 312 was owned by a gentleman in France, and while Gordon could use it for timeshare purposes, he could not sell that specific space. He quickly offered us the outright ownership of an apartment on the first level instead; however, we wanted to stay with No. 312. For some reason, the ground level always seems vulnerable to me—like possible theft and definitely creepy bugs. Maybe even *ratas*.

He assured us that it would all get straighten out.

*   *   *

Continuing our quest to learn about our surroundings, we read about a unique waterfall called El Limon with a height of over 150 feet, located high in the hill country between Samaná and Las Terrenas. The brochure that John showed us described El Limon as wondrous, reportedly 300 meters above sea level with a 45-meter drop that ended in a deep, swimmable pool of crystal clear water. We agreed that it was a must-do adventure, so, with swimsuits in our tote bags, we rented a *mucho mejor* car and headed out once again for the eastern end of the island.

Driving along Calle Principal, we passed through small villages, endless sugarcane, and coconut plantations. I asked Bill to pull over for a minute where a Haitian man was cutting sugarcane. Handing him a package of peanut butter crackers, I said, "Por favor," pointing at a stalk he had just cut with his machete. Back in the car, I sucked on the fibrous flesh and suddenly knew why so often we had seen children doing the same. The sugarcane tasted mildly like maple just as it came from the tree.

We came upon a funeral procession. Men, women, and children were walking along the road, singing hymns with arms filled with flowers while the coffin rested in a wagon with a horse pulling it, the pastor leading. We stopped, waiting for them to pass, and then *they* stopped, while a small group of cows crossed the road.

We all remained awake on this trip as we drove the busy road past small clutches of houses where the wash was drying on barbed-wire fencing. People in a constant flow were walking to visit one another after church, not bothered by potholes or the roar and dust or fumes from motor bikes zooming by with, at times, an entire family on board.

Families enjoyed the day together in front of their homes. Old men sporting spotless shirts sat in chairs, smoking, playing cards or dominos; women, in their housedresses, cooking in the yard on stoves fired by wood scraps and dried leaves. Ashes fluttered like moths into the almond trees. Young girls wore crispy clean party dresses, their lovely white teeth flashed as they swept dirt pathways through their yard with grass brooms, or braided each other's hair. Grandmothers held the babies. A *true* free-range chicken came running out of the front doorway of one apricot-colored house with sun-bleached green shutters.

Upon reaching Samaná, Bill turned northward; following signs that appeared in abundance along the road heralding guided tours to El Limon. By the map that John was doggedly studying, it appeared that we still had a ways to go, so we continued up the winding mountain road.

Suddenly, a man appeared on the right excitedly waving a red bandana at us. We pulled over only to find out through dual English and Spanish that he was touting a guided tour through the woods to El Limon. His enthusiasm was contagious, so I asked Bill to turn into the crude entrance to a small open field with a rustic lean-to for horses off to the side. I heard the soft clopping of their hooves as they milled about in the pen, snuffling and neighing as if in quiet conversation.

Grinning from ear to ear, the bandana man and three other eager-faced Dominicans standing next to some scrawny horses, said, *No problema, Mama, veinte minutos. Cincuenta pesos.* I, the interpreter, said to my compatriots: "Twenty minutes to the falls and only fifty pesos each."

"Let's do it" Ann shouted, leaping out of the car, always ready for adventure.

They asked if we wanted to ride their horses. We declined, being four, near-sixty-five year olds in good physical shape. We asked where we could change into our bathing suits to swim in the pool beneath the falls. The head guide, Dominico, said in his broken English, "Never mind, Mama, we have *baño* at El Limon, you change there. Twenty minutes." We paid in advance; 100 pesos per couple . . . a bargain at $12 US.

So off we went, following Dominico and his assistant along the narrow, twisting pathway, joking that they had brought two horses along anyway. Dominico pointed out the flora and fauna, as we passed grapefruit, avocado, lemon, mango, papaya, and banana trees all along the way. Walking through the dark tangle of vegetation, my legs brushed fragrances from unidentified bushes.

Thirty minutes later, as it turned out, we were still not there, and Bill decided to ride one of the horses who sported a saddle made of burlap crocheted with 4-inch pieces of multi-colored rags. Not much of a cushion he realized later.

About this time into our serpentine trek, there was little conversation, only huffing and puffing, Ann still leading the pack. Up and down hills we trudged, through steep, narrow twists and gullies, over reddish lava stones imbedded in the pathway—slippery and sharp—and then a run of flat terrain when my legs could stop trembling briefly. Geckos skittered from the shadows, watching with unblinking eyes.

Every so often there were stretches of what Dominico referred to as *chocolata*—i.e. mud three inches deep, softened by brief early morning torrential rain showers, topped frequently with neat piles of glistening horse droppings which mixed in rapidly as our feet acted like eggbeaters. We stumbled through each patch as it oozed over the top of our sneakers, pulling shoe away from heel. The sucking was so strong that it felt like I couldn't keep up with my own forward motion.

Finally, *an hour* after our first steps into the tropical jungle, we arrived, exhausted, at a hut near the top of the falls where they sold drinks and, of course, had a ticket seller—only 10 pesos more to go the rest of the way down a vertical trail to the foot of the falls. No more than ten minutes ahead.

Bill followed Ann who had already charged forward, bounding, surefooted, down the last lap of the slippery trip . . . like a gazelle. John and I watched them disappear, shaking our heads. I figured that I had no choice but to continue since we had come this far, however I seriously questioned Dominico's ability to guesstimate time, and my own ability to know my limitations.

Down, down, John and I went, grabbing at branches to slow the pace, trying to follow our eager mates over the steepest passage yet. When we arrived at the bottom, there was the spectacular waterfall, 155 feet above, cascading and thundering off the edge of the world into the large pool right there before us. The afore-referenced *baño,* where we could change into our bathing suits, was a simple two-sided lean-to against the canyon wall, but at this point, feeling hot and mucky, modesty wasn't an issue.

Within minutes we were floating on our backs in the cold fresh water, looking up at the falls—the rich green forest and cloudless sky—feeling the spray needling our faces like the freezing sting of hail. I stared up at the plunging water, the way it flashed and held the sun, hundreds of iridescent rainbows like a swarm of dragonflies. The *chocolata* washed away and our body temperatures quickly returned to normal. Finally, Dominico signaled that it was time to go. Reluctantly, we changed back into our hiking gear and ascended the path to the head of the falls. I wrapped my wet bathing suit around my head to keep it cool.

The trip back seemed much shorter since Dominico took hold of my hand: "*Vamos, Mama,*" he'd said, and hauled me over hill and dale and *mucho chocolata,* back to our car, which I was relieved to see was still there. Now, Bill rode the horse like John Wayne and probably thought he was. The blazing sun flickering through the trees was low in the west.

With spirits high, we threw our chocolata-encrusted shoes into the trunk, turned on the air-conditioner and headed toward Las Terrenas, where we planned to spend the night. I noticed Bill was squirming in the driver's seat as he drove.

"How ya doin' Mr. Wayne?" I asked. The look he gave me said it all.

*   *   *

While imbibing at the pool bar three days before we were to leave for home, we overheard Gordon pitching his *latest* timeshare sales scheme at a nearby table . . . "one week a year for forty years at the Windsurf Resort." Bill and I, thinking that it could possibly take that long to acquire a *título* to No. 312, decided that forty years would do us just fine. So, after a bit of *new* negotiations, it was settled that the cash payment we had previously made for the ownership of unit No. 312, would be applied to the purchase of . . . *sixteen weeks a year of timeshare for forty years.* That would allow us to stay at the Windsurf Resort four months every winter until doomsday and then our six kids could split up the remaining time among them . . . a good arrangement, we thought, much safer than waiting for a title that might never materialize.

*   *   *

After returning home, we found that many friends and family members *believed* our glowing stories about the DR and suggested that they'd "sure like to visit sometime." So I wrote the following letter to be given to anyone who did visit:

Dear Visitor:

We have a one-bedroom apartment, No. 312, on the third floor (walk up) at the Windsurf Resort in a town called Cabarete. It also has a pull out couch in the living room and a full kitchen set up. Very basic living. A balcony looks out over an artfully landscaped central common area and the swimming pool. Maid service cleans up every day . . . the women are very sweet. It is appropriate to leave 500 pesos/wk at the end of your stay.

I suggest that you leave any good jewelry at home. Just wear fun stuff, and do not flash large amounts of money. The Dominicans in Cabarete are wonderful, friendly, caring people, but there are always those who are desperately poor and look for opportunities.

You fly into the Puerto Plata airport on American or Continental. As you enter the main room of the airport, go to your left to a counter where you must fill out an entrance form and pay $10 US per person. Be sure to keep the receipt, as you need to turn it back in when you leave. (They also offer a welcoming cup of rum punch there. Beware; it hits you as soon as you enter the heat of the day). Customs will check your passports and you then proceed to get your luggage. You are subject to a possible inspection before exiting the airport.

The taxi fare will be $25+/- US. Be sure to add a tip. The trip is 20 +/- minutes depending on traffic. You will go through the town of Sosuá on the way. You may want to return there for a visit to look around. Ask Socorro (our friend at the front desk) about excursions. There are three ways to do short distance travel; taxi, moto concho *(on the back of a motorbike) or* guagua *(vans that go back and forth between Cabarete and Sosuá . . . you hail it to stop and they literally stuff you in and for 10 pesos will take you on a wild ride to Sosuá).*

Windsurf Resort is right across the street from the beautiful horseshoe-shaped beach where there are several restaurants to choose from. The sun is intense. Be sure to slather yourself in lotion. It's easy walking to everything—grocery store, pharmacy, and little shops. It's romantic to walk the beach at night (take a flashlight with you). There are water activities like windsurfing and kite sailing, (ask at the front desk to get a discount or free hour of instruction on the beach). There are a lot of excursions that one can sign up for, if you get bored with the pool, the beach, and eating . . . ha ha. We like to do our food shopping at Janet's mercado: turn right out of Windsurf and walk about 1/4 mile and it is across the street (on the water side). A little bit beyond Janet's, on the same side is a small restaurant called Claro's, good for breakfast or lunch.

Weekdays, you'll see school children all dressed in blue-as-the-sky shirts and tan pants and skirts. There are two sessions each day. The staff at the Windsurf Resort is great and will help you with anything. The restaurant connected to the hotel has good food and is reasonable. Gordon Gannon is the owner of the Windsurf and is a friend whom we have known since 1990s.

It is safe to brush your teeth with tap water, but for all drinking, do use bottled water which you can get at the desk or at Janet's. BE CAREFUL CROSSING THE MAIN STREET— LOOK BOTH WAYS THREE TIMES AND THEN RUN! Some people have been hit by speeding vehicles.

Our Canadian friends, Ian and Lynn, live 150 yards east on the beach and would be most friendly to you. There are ATM machines in Cabarete where you can use your US cards for cash (it comes out in pesos) or you can exchange dollars for pesos at the front desk. There is a medical center a couple of blocks from the hotel with a German doctor who speaks English.

Have fun and say: Hola, *to all you meet, then point to yourself and say:* Amigo de Bill y Julie. *Have a fantastic visit.*

The Windsurf Resort, Cabarete,
Dominican Republic
* 809-571-0718 * Unit No. 312

Socorro, Jose, and Windsurf Staff

Doug and Marguerite – Castle Club

Windsurf Resort

"Chocolata"

SIETE

1999 - ADVENTURES

This year, we went directly to the Windsurf Resort and were greeted by Socorro with *Bienvenidos, amigos!* Our reserved apartment No. 312 was ready and waiting for us, where Elizabeth had placed a bouquet of pink bougainvillea on the table and formed swans on the bed from towels to welcome us.

Before leaving New Hampshire, we had been horrified to hear about the devastation caused when Hurricane Georges struck the DR in September of 1998. It was a large and furious Cape Verde hurricane that pounded the southern and central portions of the country, nearing the threshold of category-five intensity. The torrential rain in the mountainous country to the north and west of Barahona had rapidly filled every mountain stream to overflowing, causing not only widespread severe flooding, but terrifying mud slides that inundated complete villages as the liquefied mixture of debris, vegetation, animals and humans raced toward the sea.

Three hundred Dominicans were reported dead, while in actuality thousands of backcountry people had been swept away—a great many families never found, buried forever. Georges destroyed or damaged 300,000 homes in total. The storm also wiped out small farms in the mountains, leaving the survivors with no means of supporting themselves. There simply had not been time enough to notify the residents and certainly no way to evacuate them, even if they had been forewarned.

Bill, who had been working with Habitat for Humanity for several years, decided that we should "give a house" to the Dominican Republic, and through the Habitat International office in Americus, Georgia, he requested that our donation be directed to Barahona where a large housing project was already underway. Ever since we started fleeing winters in New England, I stopped shopping for Hanukkah and Christmas gifts for our children and grandchildren and started sending checks to be spent for the benefit of each family. This year, instead of a check, we decided to give to each member of our family, "pictures" of windows, doors, roofs, refrigerator, stove, sinks, toilets, cabinets, etc. superimposed on the headlines of the tragic hurricane, with a reminder of how much we have to be grateful for.

When visiting our nine-year old grandson, Elan, he disappeared upstairs to his room, returning minutes later with two dollars. "Grammie and Grampy, I want to contribute." We choked up a bit and could only say, "Thank you, it will help."

*   *   *

Soon after we had arrived in Cabarete in January, we rented a car for a trip to Barahona with Ann and John enthusiastically joining us in the adventure. Bill had arranged to meet with the Habitat International representatives who were in charge of the ongoing project. We wanted to see the area first hand, as well as to actually help build the house our family had donated.

To reach Barahona, which is in the southwestern part of the country, we drove over the mountains early enough to see mist that hung in wet sheets along the valley under a band of bright blue sky. Following the coast southwest from Santo Domingo, the road curved along the Caribbean coastline stretching almost to the Haitian border. A seven-hour drive from Cabarete. The road was in fairly good shape compared to the one that runs through Cabarete, although there were some pretty scary winding turns high on the cliff tops where the view was spectacular.

The improvised city of Barahona itself would not be too appealing to tourists, even before the storm. There wasn't much to offer aesthetically in the way of a typical seaside town: no main beach for sunbathing, no restaurants with "safe" food for vacationers. But then, that was not our mission.

Needing a place to stay, John, who could always be depended on to sleuth out a situation, found a hotel that was open even though it looked deserted. The rooms were basic. They seemed clean, but far from even three-star quality, and of course, no air conditioning. The ninety foot long lobby was, I imagine, a throwback to better times—huge marble columns that reached up to support a splendidly cloud-painted ceiling, tiled floors, and a run of French doors on one side, opening out toward the bay. The other walls were adorned with wonderful, colourful art depicting local scenes of daily life.

The first morning, John, Bill and I entered the lobby where we observed Ann standing on a chair, straightening some of the art work that was hanging unevenly on the walls. We didn't comment as she got down from the chair and joined us at the café at the far end of the lobby where we *cautiously* ate breakfast. After the waiter took our order, he proceeded to open the French doors and an aggressive gust of fresh sea air burst into the lobby tilting all the pictures on the walls that Ann had just straightened. After a moment of hesitation, we all burst out laughing—Ann perhaps the most.

It was in Barahona that I first heard about Larimar. Our waiter showed us a jar filled with light blue stones which he wished to sell. Guess who bought them? He told us that a Peace Corps volunteer, Miguel Méndez, when looking for petro glyphs and pictograms from the days of the Taino Indian settlers, discovered a pale blue-colored stone while exploring caves in Barahona with his daughter, Larissa. Natives, who believed the unique gemstone came from the sea, called the variant of pectolite, *Blue Stone*. But actually, it was formed by volcanoes millions of years before. Miguel blended his young daughter's name and the Spanish word for sea, *mar,* to form the name *Larimar*. Today, along with Amber, Larimar has been made into jewelry and sold all over the DR. The very next day, Ann was thrilled to find a precious piece of Larimar on the beach, which she later had made into a ring.

We were met at the hotel later that morning by our hosts from Habitat International, who drove us to the building site and introduced us to Rosita, the widowed mother of seven for whom

Habitat was building the house. Before Hurricane Georges, Rosita had lived in the mountains and had supported her family with her own business of selling herbs and charcoal. I could only imagine what it would be like being one of seven children living together with just your mother in a tin house the size of our family room. One toilet, one stove, no hot water, no TV, no phone, and only two beds.

Like so many others, we were told, her home was totally destroyed and many became depressed and apathetic. However, in Rosita's case, she worked hard at keeping her family together by making charcoal and selling it. Her inner strength and spirit were inspirational. For the home we are building, she will pay a no-interest mortgage of about $500 peso per month for 5 years. As the money comes in, Habitat rolls it over into another house. A great system.

When disaster strikes anywhere, the Red Cross, my most favorite organization, is the first to help. But they can't build houses. What I like about Habitat is that it's a direct charity where all the money goes right into building or renovation of homes. We learned that the standard Habitat home in the DR was 6 meters by 8 meters with a flat roof, a set size for economy of construction. As time goes on, families can elect to add a second story, a porch, or another bedroom.

Everyone is a volunteer, except the cement mixer mason and the electrician, both of whom are hired to work and each paid $14 a day. For the next several days at the site of Rosita's house, we four worked alongside Rosita, her friends, and the volunteers, helping to build the flat solid concrete roof. I couldn't carry water or stone in the women's bucket brigade, but, boy, could I shovel sand for the cement mixer. Gravel and sand, Ann and I shoveled away. Bill and John were part of the cement-to-roof process. Each day, in the gruelling sun. And did we ever sleep like babies each night. We were all pooped.

Next to the sand pile, I saw a spiny looking cactus that seemed to cling precariously to life in this parched region. It had pretty, white flowers on its plump water-retaining pads. Rosita said it is called the Prickly Pear Cactus, known among the locals as *tuna*. The fruit is very hard to handle, but is considered quite a delicacy. Carefully, Bill cut one open for me to taste . . . it was delicious, like a mango.

There were to be three small bedrooms, a bathroom, a living room, and an outdoor kitchen. The process for constructing the roof was basic: mix cement on the ground, shovel it into a bucket, tie a rope to the handle, and raise it to the roof where it was dumped into a wheelbarrow, then wheeled to the edge of the ever-expanding poured slab. Concrete blocks, cement, iron rods, sand, and gravel were the materials used for all the houses in order to withstand future hurricane threats, usually threatening from July to November. These materials could be easily purchased in the country, although at prices far greater than Rosita could afford.

We took many photos in which the workers posed enthusiastically with dirt-smeared faces and happy smiles. It was Rosita's task and contribution to organize feeding the volunteers—around thirty of us. The women banded together, cooking large pots of rice and red beans with chunks of fresh pineapples added at the last minute. When I went with them to help carry the food, one woman proudly pointed out a picture of an American flag on the wall of her house.

Rosita made a plaque before we left. The names of each of our children and grandchildren were listed, with her promise: "You will always be welcome in this little house." When it was time for us to leave Barahona, there were hugs and exclamations of *muchas gracias* and *vaya con Dios.*

The trip back to Cabarete seemed much shorter even though we all were in pain from blisters and aching muscles that we hadn't heard from in many a year. A funny episode occurred on the highway as we approached Puerto Plata. About two miles outside the city, there was an enormous traffic circle. We counted at least eight entrances and exits spinning off and on with all signs in Spanish. Naturally. The terrain was flat, desert-like, causing Bill to be unsure which turn to take. We had entered the circle in the midst of heavy commuter traffic and around we went—again and again. Bill's face was getting red and we were all craning our necks to read the signs when we saw a man in an old rusted truck waving at us, yelling, *Adonde?* In unison, we yelled back: Cabarete! His truck roared in front of us as he signaled us to follow. Halfway around again, he pointed at an off ramp, but not in time for us to take it. So around we went once more with our guide still in the lead. Bill honked like crazy when, this time, we exited the circle. Bill pulled over as soon as possible and said, "Your turn to drive, Johnny, I'm dizzy."

We arrived back in Cabarete with the feeling of accomplishment and satisfaction. The building of the Habitat house in Barahona had been exhilarating.

*   *   *

After a few days of relaxation and muscle restoration, John suggested that we plan an overnight whale-watching trip to Samaná Bay. Although somewhat reluctant due to my food poisoning experience in Samaná, I agreed to go. Off we went, early in the morning, in another rental car. Bill drove and John rode pothole-shotgun, while Ann and I held down the back seat. We had had a hearty breakfast before leaving, as I was determined not to stop for food along the highway. I wanted to drink in the magnificent natural surroundings of the Dominican countryside.

We drove past boundless panoramic views of mountains in the distance to the south, with braids of smoke that rose from the foothills and every shade of green glowed in the lush fields and groves of coconut palms. Frequent brief rain showers explained the luxuriant vegetation. Cattle grazed in open fields, which were separated by live-tree *Peñon* fences with barbed wire woven throughout their branches. Roque had shown us how we could simply cut off a branch of a *Peñon*, jam it into the ground and it would take hold, putting out roots and sprouting leaves within weeks. Wish I could do that in New Hampshire with fruit trees and paper white birches.

Every so often, the highway ran right along the ocean where endless beaches, usually unoccupied, would appear with white-capped waves crashing as they flowed to shore. Then we would pass through a run of small homes barely ten feet from the road's edge where spanking-white laundry hung out on barbed wire fences, while goats, chickens, and burros grazed peacefully in the small side yards. Young children looked up from their play to wave as our car sped by.

By our standards, the poverty was staggering in the DR. More often than not, there were two families living in one house, including grandparents, parents, and children sharing beds. However, and fortunately, in the country, people had all the food they could eat, roofs over their heads, plenty of water—and always, a ready smile.

Samaná City was reportedly settled around 1820 by two shiploads of freed American slaves and, to this day, many residents speak English as a first language. This worked well for us, since we had procrastinated year after year about learning decent conversational Spanish.

Arriving in Samaná around eleven thirty, we had just enough time to grab a bite to eat at a dockside *caferteria* that offered *casaba,* a thin flat bread made of yucca, filled with avocado, tomatoes, and other crunchy vegetables.

Upon boarding the whale watching boat along with about thirty other sightseers, everyone was directed to put on a life jacket and sit on the seats along each side of the open cockpit. The guide then told us to hold out our hands placed together, open at the top, as she proceeded to walk past us, dropping in a seasick pill. It reminded me of the game we used to play as children: *Button, button, who's got the button?* She was followed by another woman with a tray of cups filled with water to wash the pills down. Like children, we dutifully obeyed.

In spite of the medication, yours truly started to feel nauseous a half-hour out, and so while everyone else was leaning on the edge to watch more closely, I was concentrating on the floor of the boat. Nonetheless, I was listening to the guide when he said that although their name would suggest otherwise, humpbacks did not actually have a humped back. It only looked that way when they surfaced out of the water with arched backs. Also I remember he said that they have *two* blowholes rather than one.

When everyone cheered, I looked up quickly just as one incredible humpback rose out of the water with grace—like a gentle giant.

The guide went on to say that we were in one of the largest breeding sanctuaries in the world. Every year between January and March, thousands of whales migrate from their feeding grounds in the North Atlantic to these relatively shallow waters protected by coral reefs where they reproduced.

We learned that humpbacks eat close to a ton of food a day in the north, which is stored in the form of fat. Consequently, they do not need to eat much during their stay in these waters. The newly born calves drink 50 gallons of milk a day produced by the mother, allowing them to grow big enough to survive the journey back to the feeding grounds of the north. All this talk about eating made my stomach churn even more so, and I was happy when we docked—back on terra firma. Yes, very happy.

*   *   *

It was a twenty-five minute drive from the wharf to The Gran Bahía Príncipal, a Victorian-style, elegant as a palace, five-star hotel located on the beach on the Samaná peninsula. We had decided to splurge by living in luxury for one night. And, oh my, what luxury—a pristine surprise for nature lovers such as us.

As we entered our lavishly appointed living room, I looked across the expansive space through open shuttered doors that led to a balcony overlooking a large swimming pool, formal landscaping, and a dazzling view over the sea out to Cayo Levantado Island. Ann was doing some kind of a dance across the startling black and white tile floor.

After completing our tour of these grand quarters and then unpacking, we descended the wide curved granite stairway from our suite to the dining room where we were greeted with aromas of an elaborate array of exquisite cuisine—great food by any other name. Being an all-inclusive arrangement, we ate ourselves into autointoxication, and tottered off to bed on the early side of the night.

*   *   *

We had invited daughter Lynn and family to visit us but as it turned out, only Emily and Sarah made the trip. Because they were 12 and 14, a parental letter of permission to enter and especially for an unaccompanied exit from the country needed to be signed by the Dominican Counsel in Boston. Lynn planned to take a quick trip to Boston to take care of it. Had I been there, I would have warned her that *nothing is ever simple*, a truth I keep in mind at all times. Upon arriving at the office, she was told there was no one there who spoke English and she would have to wait. After two hours of sitting patiently, she watched as a group of people left the office, obviously for lunch. Extremely frustrated, Lynn grabbed a quick sandwich and returned for another long wait. Finally, seeing that she simply was not going to leave, someone signaled her up to the counter and with a flourish, signed the papers. Her next task was to arrange with the airline for an escort because Emily and Sarah were under aged. That apparently went a lot smoother. It was fortunate that she had gone to the trouble of airport supervision, because winter icing on the plane forced a re-route to an unexpected stop in Puerto Rico, and then changing planes to the DR. American Airlines stayed in touch with their parents throughout the changes, for which we were all grateful. However, the girls confessed later that the tags around their necks as UNACCOMPANIED MINORS made them feel more vulnerable than less.

When we met the girls at the airport in Puerto Plata, our sweet granddaughters were all smiles . . . obviously taking the world traveler mantle in stride.

They were easy guests since they loved to play board games with us, frolic on the beach, swim laps in the pool, listen to stories by René and Sandra, and sleep late in the morning. That was a bit of a problem because they shared the couch that opened to a double bed right in the middle of the No. 312 living room. Bill and I had to tiptoe around till almost noon.

Two days before their departure, the girls, who both have long golden hair, spent four hours sitting by the pool while having their hair braided by talented Haitian ladies. The girls looked very different from when they arrived as they boarded the plane for home with glowing sun-pinked faces, a myriad of tight beaded braids adorning their heads, and a touch of sadness to be parting in their smiles. It had been a fun visit and they told us that they had kept the braids in, sand and all, for nearly a week after they returned to school.

*   *   *

Every weekday I saw children, looking newly laundered and pressed, passing by the Windsurf on the way to *escuela,* dressed in school uniforms. The young girls walked hand-in-hand while chatting away and giggling at the boys who were running ahead, showing off. They were eager groups going to and from school for the morning session—only blocks beyond our hotel—and then a different set of children for the afternoon session. Most of them came from the *barrios*—large communities where grievously poor Dominicans lived. All public school teachers were hired and paid for by the national government, not the local government.

The one-story cement-block school building was set back thirty feet from the street with a front play yard of packed dirt, and only one tree to provide some shade. Yet I could often hear the children's playful, carefree voices lilting from the playground to our balcony.

Once on our way to shop at Janet's *super mercado,* we stopped by the school while the kids were at recess. I pointed to myself, saying that I was a *maestro de Boston* — (I figured Boston would be better known to her than New Hampshire). The teacher, who spoke no English but understood, beckoned me to follow her inside to the one open room roughly twenty feet by twenty, with three shuttered windows facing out to the street. There were double chairs attached to each of the fifteen desks that were scattered around the room and one large blackboard on the wall behind the teacher's desk. I didn't see any other teaching materials, and except for what looked like a manual on the teacher's desk, *there were no other books.*

No books.

Having been an educator for 35 years, the bleakness of this school saddened me and immediately I pictured our next trip to Cabarete with an extra suitcase filled with children's books for this little *escuela.*

Back at the Windsurf, Bill and I asked Socorro about the Dominican schools. She said that most rural schools like the one in Cabarete, were *insuficiente.* She then went on to talk about The Dominican Republic Education and Mentoring (DREAM)

Project centered in Cabarete, a nonprofit organization whose aim was to "provide quality education for children living in rural areas and other communities like Cabarete."

DREAM was supported by combining volunteerism, international awareness, and community involvement. She said that they are sustained through contributions of time, talent, funds, materials, and supplies from individuals, foundations, and local businesses. Even so, Socorro sends her daughter to a private school in Sosúa and much of her salary went to pay for it. "Without a good education," she told us, "you don't get anywhere in the Dominican Republic."

On the information counter, I found a brochure next to a donation box that stated the DREAM Project's mission: *"It is our vision that all children born in the Dominican Republic have the opportunity to receive an education and learn to their full potential. It is our hope that our efforts can be multiplied to allow the opportunity for every child's gifts and challenges to be met with support nationwide. It is our goal to break the cycle and change people's destinies. It is our dream that the world will be a better place for the children and families of the next generation."*

Their goals for the Dominican children truly made me hopeful.

In further reading, we learned what a fantastic organization the DREAM Project actually was. It operated summer camps, youth groups, preschools, and training facilities. Working in partnership with the Dominican Government, the United Nations, the U.S. Peace Corps, USAID, and non-governmental organizations, they employed local teachers and administrators, and brought in international volunteers who taught in classrooms, libraries, and laboratories. I was excited about The DREAM Project and have contributed to it enthusiastically each year since we first heard about it.

And then . . . Louise, the one-woman Canadian dynamo entered the scene, who, strictly by her own initiative, raised money and acquired donations in her hometown of Winnipeg, Canada for the schoolchildren in Cabarete and the surrounding villages. Louise and her husband, Vince, arrived each year with suitcases and boxes filled with school supplies. She called her effort: *Project Dominican School Friends.*

Over an eleven-year span, Louise told me that she had collected total donations in excess of $70,000 by dint of her own fundraising efforts, which included both letters and personal appearances at numerous organizations in Winnipeg. Other interesting totals were: 3,147 uniforms, 3,047 schoolbags, 7,000 pencils, 6,708 toothbrushes, 16 wheelchairs, 3,420 boxes of crayons, and 160 suitcases filled with a myriad of miscellaneous supplies and educational materials. I was beyond impressed. Just think of what one person can do.

For the uniforms, which cost about $20 US, and which are *required* by the Government in order for a child to attend school, Louise contracted with a business in Sosúa and had them made to order. She was doubly proud to have not only provided many uniforms, but to also to have created jobs for the local business and its employees.

"In addition to providing these items to schools and

education," Louise continued, "we have donated $8,060.00 in cash to the Martina Orphanage in Puerto Plata over the past five years." She then added, "This project has been a powerful experience for Vince and me—one that has changed my life forever."

What an awesome woman with the sparkling blue eyes.

On one particular visit, Bill and I assisted Louise in setting up a luncheon at the Ocean Taste Restaurant, where over forty children from various villages ate their fill, sang, and laughed, while receiving school supplies. I helped hand out some of the gifts that Louise had purchased with donations. It may have been the first time for some of these kids to ever receive a wrapped gift, but unlike me who might have carefully unwrapped and saved the paper, they tore away the colorful paper in their excitement, and delighted in whatever was inside. Unspoiled and genuinely pleased with what they got, the children crushed around Louise as though she were a saint, kissing her with ice cream smeared faces.

For me, it was uplifting just to take that small part in Louise's dedication to the schoolchildren of Cabarete and the Dominican Republic.

Julie Shoveling for HFH

Rosita and Family

Louise's Luncheon for Children

Sarah and Emily in Braids

OCHO

2000-2002 - REAL ESTATE

Bill and I, now both officially retired, were looking forward to a three-month stay when we arrived in Cabarete on a picture-perfect afternoon in December of 2000. After twenty-four years of launching six kids and pursuing our careers, we would now have plenty of leisure time to move into a new and exciting phase of our relationship. We were both ecstatic at the thought although we would miss Ann and John who were not planning to retire for several more years. After heartfelt greetings by our friends on the Windsurf Resort staff, we settled into No. 312. Eagerly, we decided to get reacquainted with Cabarete by taking a stroll downtown before dinner.

Friends had written for us to expect drastic changes due to a huge influx of tourists. It almost came as a shock when we realized that Cabarete was no longer undiscovered. The continued lure of the excellent conditions for windsurfing and world-class competitions jump-started more competitors and vacationers wanting more accommodations, restaurants, and entertainment. By 2000, Cabarete had exploded.

Of course, we knew that that would happen as soon as telephone and internet services became available. Yes, there was an internet café right in the middle of Cabarete now, but so smoke-filled that I knew it would take a dire emergency for me to even step inside. Bill did brave the smoke to check emails and stock market updates.

As opposed to all-inclusive resorts where the amenities were enclosed and guests were secure, Cabarete catered to more adventuresome people, like us, who wanted not to be isolated from Dominican life and its people, but to be in the heart of it.

The previously wide-open beach setting that had first defined Cabarete lined with the original old wooden homes had become a compact row of little shops and restaurants sandwiched in-between small hotels and guesthouses. It was a shock to us comparing this Cabarete to the "sleepy little fishing village" that had greeted us in the 1980s. But it didn't take long to adjust. I appreciated dependable electricity and "safe" restaurants in which to eat, but more than anything, I loved to see the Dominican people earning money, getting ahead.

A scene that immediately plunged us back into the hum of Cabarete was when a dented, wheezing car stopped in the middle of the road beside us, music at ear-splitting pitch, while the driver got out to embrace a friend. This legendary friendliness is what enchanted us with the people and the charm of this alluring destination.

*   *   *

Our entrepreneurial son Steve had alerted us, after his recent visit to Cabarete with his family, to watch for waterfront property for sale, as he was quite sure he had seen a sign being put up on a fence when he was on his way to the airport. When we crossed the street, there it was—an eight-foot high, corrugated tin wall blocking the view of the beach—all four hundred feet of it, with several prominent signs saying: *Ocean Front Land for Sale* . . . in English. It extended from the Pequeño Refugio—a hotel immediately across the street from the Windsurf Resort—up the beach, to the Mariposa Restaurant, where we had decided to have a sundowner drink. In Spanish, mariposa means butterfly, and on the winding stairway leading to luxury suites on the second floor and overlooking the indoor Mariposa restaurant, was the most enormous multi-colored mural of a butterfly, beautiful and graceful. An enchanting sight we always enjoyed when frequenting their breakfast buffet with Ann and John.

As we walked to a table on the terrace, I saw a young man gesticulating and talking earnestly with an older couple. "I bet he's selling real estate," I commented to Bill, who already had a conspiratorial gleam in his eyes.

After ordering a bahama mama, I excused myself to visit the *baño*. Hesitating at the young man's table, I asked, boldly: "Are you in sales?"

"Yes," he responded with a charming look and accent that sounded a cross between Spanish and German. "Real estate. Are you interested?"

"Always," I told him and moved on.

A short while later, Bernie, our instant new friend sat down with us and launched into his pitch saying that the land cordoned off by the metal fence contained five lots, all for sale. *Right on the ocean*. He was young, early twenties, very personable, and extremely enthusiastic.

Guess who made an offer on the middle lot after a brief negotiation?

Hans, the property owner, was a Swiss businessman who, at the moment had a cash obligation on another matter which was so urgent that he asked us to finalize the sale within three days. It was incredibly exciting. What we purchased was one of his center lots, sixty-five feet of waterfront land upon which was an existing 45 ft. square building. The front was set back twenty feet from the ocean and the rear, twenty feet from a high stone wall along the road which worked as a good sound barrier (always important to Bill, my acoustical engineer). The house, an adjunct to the former Cabarete Beach Hotel next door, was completely furnished. It had a common room in the center surrounded by five bedrooms, each with a bathroom. Our vacation now took on a whole new purpose. We were on a roll.

*   *   *

Days flew by with all kinds of thoughts rushing through our minds and sketches galore going from one extreme to another. We finally settled on the idea of leasing the building as is to the owner of the BIC windsurfing rental operation for one year. In the meantime, long-range plans for this investment property took shape. We would build a new, six-unit building at the end of that lease. Hugh put us in touch with an architect who started to develop Bill's plans and we worked out an agreement to have Windsurf Resort, i.e. Gordon, manage the future building as time-share units.

*   *   *

While we were firmly entrenching ourselves for a future life in Cabarete, the fun of living at the Windsurf Resort continued. We had more and more visitors. Nancy and Doug, neighbors near our Lakehouse in New Hampshire, came to see what had gotten us so excited and they quickly became regulars. Nancy went so far as to consider starting a business of making and selling dresses to the native Dominicans or hot fudge sundaes with her secret chocolate recipe, while Doug reveled in body surfing and playing tennis. Never a dull moment with them.

Maria had taught us how to play Mexican Train with a set of Double-12 dominoes. It was loads of fun and we hooked every new visitor we had into playing. One day we played Mexican Train on the beach and foolishly left the set there while we swam for a short time, only to have it stolen. Fortunately, Nancy and Doug, who were about to visit again, offered to bring along a new set. Doug, who doesn't usually play games at all, let us know *clearly* just how heavy the set was and that he had to carry it the entire trip.

Jean and Dick, old-time mutual friends of ours and Ann and John's, shared a captivating evening with dinner at La Puntilla de Piergiorgio restaurant, situated on a cliff edge over Sosúa Bay. Attached was a grand, white clapboard hotel with a wraparound verandah adorned with ornamental gingerbread, characteristic of Sosúa's glory days in the Victorian era. Known as a honeymoon destination, the grand marbled foyer led out to terraced gardens laced with pathways leading to the outdoor dining overlooking the bay below. Waiters in crisp white outfits glided by like moths flitting among the many guests. Each table lamp was covered with pink cloth casting an enchanting romantic glow. We sixty plus-year-old folks admitted to each other how it carried us all back to earlier days. Quintessential of what drew us to the DR.

*   *   *

The second time our daughter Julie B. and family came on vacation, they arrived the afternoon of New Year's Eve, having brought with them gifts that would be way beyond the hopes of most young Dominicans.

Our son-in-law Ari had returned home after their first visit to Cabarete more fully aware of the sore lack of baseball equipment. As an involved parent of Little League in Portsmouth, he put out an appeal to all the local baseball leagues for any used or obsolete equipment. The front porch of Sherburne Avenue turned into a mini-warehouse. Everything from catcher's shin guards to used uniforms began to accumulate over the summer. As winter and the pending vacation came closer, he obtained six huge duffle bags and packed them with gloves, catcher's masks, balls, and even bats. He could hardly close the zippers. They sat on his porch until their departure day. Of course, this was long before airlines charged extra for luggage—thank goodness.

Grandson Elan told us that the customs officials in Puerto Plata had looked longingly at all the baseball equipment, but since they knew who it was for, there was *no problema* with regard to paying any duty. Two taxies were needed to transport the bags and themselves to the Windsurf Resort.

We had been expecting them and were waiting in the lobby. A crowd began to gather when Bill helped unload the bags and piled them on the lobby floor. Curiosity could not be contained for long. Like wildfire, word spread to waiters, workers, and people passing by on the street that either coached a village team, or had kids who played. They all descended upon the scene. Not really getting their full credentials, but based on faith, Ari decided that then was as good a time as any, so he took charge and doled out everything from the catcher's masks to fielder's mitts. He said he could sense the need and sincerity of the men and boys, and felt that every item was well placed. In less than a half hour the huge bags were empty, and while a few went away disappointed, there was more than enough appreciation and gratitude to make the long summer's efforts worthwhile. Ari was a true American hero.

After Ari returned home, the flow of equipment continued to mount on his front porch. Our daughter Lynn and family were the next to visit us so they gathered up the additional baseball paraphernalia and delivered it in the same duffel bags. By my request, they also brought instant coffee, a deflated soccer ball and pump as a special gift for Elizabeth's brother, Luis and an Oxford English Dictionary which weighed six pounds!

*   *   *

Thinking it would be great fun for the grandchildren on New Year's Eve, we had made reservations far in advance at a new restaurant on the beach that was having a grand opening that very night. When we arrived at 8pm, the table was ready for the six of us, looking festive with candles, funny hats, and tin horns to blow at midnight. The place was packed. Happy voices and waves of Merengue music thrummed between the tables. We ordered from their brand new fancy menus, each choosing something different, and sipped at our drinks while the family started to relax after the long trip from New Hampshire earlier that day.

About one half hour later, I signaled to the waiter, asking if he could bring bread to the table since the children were squirming in their seats as well as saying they were starved. Another twenty minutes later, I suggested that Elan, nine, and Talia, age six, run down to the water's edge and back a couple of times. Keep them busy, I thought. Nearly forty minutes after that, Talia was asleep across my lap, and Elan was leaning against his mother with droopy eyes, saying that he wasn't hungry anymore.

In spite of our frustration, my sympathy went out to the waiters who were taking abuse from all the patrons. At first, I thought something might have gone wrong in the kitchen. Maybe the stove broke down, or the chef quit. Finally, after two hours of waiting, Julie B. and Ari took the children back to the house for bed, while Bill and I waited yet *another* half hour for the food, which, by then, we simply asked that it be packaged to go.

While we ate the warmed up meals for lunch the next day, Sandra told us that many people left without paying and that the grand opening had been a total disaster. We, of course, realized later that their mistake had been to have offered a complete open menu for such a crowd, instead of having only three or four dishes to choose from which they could have prepared in advance in great quantities. What a beginning for their restaurant, and what a beginning for the kids' vacation.

On their third vacation day, Julie B. and Ari, aka The Kids, decided to rent a car for a day trip to Samaná. This was great for us. Bill and I would love the fun of having Elan and Talia all to ourselves. Slathered in *mucho* sun lotion, we spent most of the day on the beach building sand castles, hunting for sea glass, and jumping the waves.

Being a mother, I slept fitfully until I heard The Kids pull in at three in the morning. I rolled over and slept soundly after that, assuming they had had a great time. Over a very late breakfast, they said that they had enjoyed the sights in Samaná. But . . . the trip back to Cabarete, which should have gotten them home around eight, was a nightmare because for some reason, the car headlights pointed straight up to the sky! They had to drive about ten miles per hour, pulling over to the side of the road the minute any headlights pierced the darkness from the opposite direction.

It had been a harrowing experience and they both had stiff necks, so I set up an appointment that afternoon with Maria for a massage. When they returned home, Julie B. was rolling her eyes, looking flushed. Maria had told her to get undressed, lie down on the table, and cover herself with a sheet. My modest daughter nervously did as she was told, and just as she was starting to relax under Maria's powerful hands, a guy just *walked right in* and began talking to Maria—who conversed with him in Spanish—while continuing to work on Julie B.'s back. She was mortified.

*   *   *

Three months after our return home that year, Bernie-the-real-estate-salesman informed us that Hans, the owner of the remaining four lots, had decided—now that our purchase was fully consummated—that he REALLY wished he had *not* sold us a center lot that now divided his remaining land, and would we be willing to change to an end lot on his property? This was after we were well into meetings and negotiations for the rental and future development.

Annoyed, but clearly seeing his point, as well as quickly reviewing potential layouts and possibilities for the alternate lot, we cancelled our lease negotiations, agreed to the swap, and chose the lot on the east end, directly across from the Windsurf

Resort. And what a spot it was. As it turned out, it was far better than the one we had first chosen.

Upon arrival that next December, we dove into the situation, again sorting between ideas and reality. Now we scrutinized our new parcel, which was flanked by the Pequeño Refugio Hotel in the process of being renovated—on the right (as you are facing the water) and Hans' soon-to-be-developed land on the other side.

Existing on our new lot was a large dilapidated ranch-style house with outer walls and roof intact, but every other imaginable thing that could have possibly been removed was gone—interior doors, fixtures from the bathrooms and kitchen. Through the open doorway on the ocean side was a 60-foot deep, junk-scattered yard that led to a crumbling *cana*-roofed *cabaña*, and then . . . on to the captivating Cabarete beach and the Atlantic Ocean. What a view . . . location times three.

We stood there hugging each other with excitement. Bill and I have always been tuned into *potential* of any kind ranging from real estate, to businesses, to publishing books, building extensions to houses, gardens, to family. Now, at ages 67 and 69 respectively, we knew we had made a good swap and a great investment.

The exchange of property ownership took several months since our attorney advised us to create two corporations—one Dominican, and one Panamanian. In the meantime, he informed us that legally we still owned the first house and its contents until the new papers were signed, and if we wanted those furnishings, to go ahead and move them to the new place. So we hired a few boys on the beach who trekked for several hours between the two houses until the first house was completely empty. Quite a scene to have these young Dominicans going back and forth—or is it forth and back?—with a chair or table or lamp held over their heads, or two boys hefting a mattress between them. Bill directed the removal while I was on the receiving end sorting items to locations of *keep* or *sell*.

Knowing that we only wanted a few of those things for ourselves, Señora Veazey, the queen of yard sales in Massachusetts and New Hampshire, decided to have one in our new "house," as it were, in the DR. We priced all items in pesos, put up signs, and asked everyone who worked at the Windsurf to tell their friends about the sale. It was a complete sell-out . . . to the walls.

For me, it was wonderful fun haggling prices in our limited Spanish, but our overall intention was to essentially give the furniture away. And we did. That was the best part. Piece after piece was carted away on someone's back, a wheelbarrow, a *moto concho*, or even a mattress on the roof of a *guagua*. For some, we held their purchase until their payday, or they found another means to take it away. There was great satisfaction in ending with an empty space. That turned out to be one of the best yard sales ever.

Hans and his wife were absolutely furious that we had "absconded" with the furnishings and literally demanded that we at least return a rattan couch and matching chair, the only items besides a few framed pictures that we had decided to keep. They obviously had spotted the set while walking the beach, as we had placed it invitingly under our now cleaned up *cabaña*. We decided to be most gracious, so they sent a young man to pick up the furniture.

*   *   *

Following several weeks of "lawyer-ing," the property became ours legally. During the waiting time, Bill transferred his designs for a six-unit two-bedroom building, slightly modified, to fit the new site and continued to work with the architect. We had chosen Hugh as our contractor, whom we knew was an accomplished builder, and it was up to him to submit the final rendition to the capitol in Santo Domingo where all official acts and permission for construction on the oceanfront occurred.

During much of its history, the Dominican Republic had been governed by strong-arm dictators who denied human rights to their citizens, particularly darker-skinned people, and there followed a swinging door of one corrupt president after another— 50 years of juntas, assignations, greed, and violence where only a few historically prominent families held most of the wealth and power.

That night, Bill saw an article in the online Dominican newsletter, *dr1.com* at the internet café, which greatly reinforced our decision to proceed. It stated that the old sugar economy had died in the 1980s when the government privatized it. The current economic strategy now relied on three sources:

1. The electronics and garment manufacturing performed in

the 43 recently established industrial free-trade zones, where more than 400 factories employed over 200,000 people— accounting for almost $1 billion in exports in 1998.

2. Tourism alone generated more than $4 billion in foreign exchange in 1999.

3. The flow of money from Dominican emigrants exceeded $3 billion.

I was staggered by those numbers, which obviously were to the credit of Leonel who had just been re-elected—now to our benefit.

So for us, it was the waiting game. Hugh and Gordon had both warned us that no one in the DR was in a hurry, especially the local self-serving politicians from whom we would have to acquire approval for the construction and a permit to proceed. Hugh told us that if we wanted to pass *mucho dinero* under the table, it might speed the process. I was glad when I saw Bill shaking his head to the contrary. It is known in the family that I am not an impatient person; I just don't like to wait.

*   *   *

Having no choice but to wait, we made a habit of taking coffee across the street from the Windsurf restaurant to greet the day in our *cabaña*. One morning, we encountered two large coconuts on the floor next to the white plastic chairs we had acquired at Janet's. Looking upward, we saw two holes in the *cana* roof, and realized that we were under attack by the towering coconut palm, nearly twenty feet above us.

Quickly, we scooted out into the yard and scrutinized the foliage. There were about ten to twelve coco-bombs poised directly above the *cabaña*. We stayed out from under until Hugh arrived. *"No problema,"* he said.

Perhaps twenty minutes later a small old-timer with gray hair, bare feet, and a short rope in his hand came into the yard from the beach. A machete hung from his belt on one side, and a rather large cloth bag on the other side, which he tossed on a chair. He smiled broadly at us, looked up, and then proceeded to *walk* up the long skinny trunk of the palm by using the rope sling and his bare feet. He made it look easy as pie.

Soon the coconuts began thumping on the ground as he swung his machete, and deftly separated and tossed one down after another. Within ten minutes, he had shimmied down and was heading for the next palm. Hugh had told us that that each of the six palms in the yard were "ready for the machete". Within an hour, the little man left with 100 pesos, and his bag filled with coconuts to be sold along the beach.

Bill reminded me that he had worked for the Rutherford Shade Tree Commission climbing and trimming trees as a teenager. He said that he was blown away by not only the technique the Dominican had used, but also by the speed with which the mission was accomplished. Bill suggested that maybe he, himself, could handle the next batch of coconuts that came ripe. His comment fell on deaf ears as we sat in the now safe shade of the *cabaña*, staring out to sea.

* * *

In the past, each year before our vacations in Cabarete, we had filled one suitcase with paperback books to assure us that we'd have plenty of reading matter while there. We then left the books at the hotel for other guests. This year, 2002, while we waited for our building permit, Bill decided to start a little book exchange— *Bill's Books*—in the vacant main room of the house. And what a hit it was. Vacationers and residents alike made regular visits to his little book store where Bill was able to schmooze to his heart's content. He salvaged an old desk, a chair, and a small bookcase from somewhere—I didn't ask where, and made up signs for the street and beach entrances.

It was then that we met Karen, a friendly young woman originally from New Hampshire, who taught school in Sosúa and now lived in the DR with her husband Richard, an investment broker. Karen and her mother, Anne, who was visiting from the States, came by one day. It didn't take long to learn that Karen loved children and animals, and was a voracious reader. When hearing that the store would be closed once we left for home, she offered to work part-time for Bill's Books—and to run it completely in the months we were not there. Thus began a great friendship and business arrangement—whatever Karen sold, the "profit" was hers. And, there would be no rent for the space. Just enjoyment.

Karen is friendly like Bill, so everyone was happy, each for their own reasons. Speaking of Karen, another wonderful quality that I so admired was her love and empathy for animals. She had adopted two horses and several dogs that had been neglected or abused; and regularly, she took it upon herself to have beach dogs and cats spayed, at her own expense. Her heart was huge.

* * *

In the meantime, Hans approached us about partnering with him in the building of the four, six-unit apartment houses on his remaining land. He even came to visit us in New Hampshire to pitch for financial backing. Although Bill spent many, many hours helping Hans with the layout, we had said no to him since we had blown our wad, so to speak, on purchasing the waterfront land. I felt badly for Bill, knowing that that kind of project really appealed to him, and for Hans, with whom we had now become friendly.

* * *

To celebrate our new acquisition as well as the arrival of Ann and John for a ten-day visit, Bill suggested we have a cocktail party in the old building before it was to be demolished. I thought it was a great idea, so we invited everyone we knew and some we didn't. There had been several prints and paintings that we had kept from the "first" house, which we now placed on the walls to give our party a festive feeling. We borrowed a long table from the Windsurf for the food and an open bar setup. The booze by far outweighed the food, a spread I had hastily put together purchased at Janet's. We borrowed a radio to liven up the party with Merengue and Bachata, fortissimo, just like the music that rang out from cars, corner stores, bars, restaurants, *guaguas*, and gas stations. It added atmosphere thanks to electricity, surreptitiously supplied via an extension cord from Pequeño Refugio, the hotel next door.

Bill had drawn a picture on a wall of how he envisioned the property *after* construction. It was the center of interest while everyone milled around in the large open-sided room and out through the yard to the *cabaña,* just as the sun lowered into the water.

I was standing under the *cabaña,* wearing a colorful Dominican skirt and a tank top, when suddenly I felt mosquitoes buzzing in bloodthirsty clouds around my head, and then up under my skirt. Just as quickly, all our guests, slapping at their arms and legs, fled the party, chased away by a barrage of mosquitoes that had apparently been just waiting for sundown. In the time it took Bill and John to grab the booze and the food, they were peppered with bites. So ended, most abruptly, our first Cabarete party. Hugh told us later that he had never seen that before and that there were probably mosquito nests buried in the sodden *cana* roof of the *cabaña.* So, right away, we asked him to replace the roof with cement, and while he was at it, could he please replace the support columns as well. And . . . make the whole *cabaña* just a little bit bigger. Which reminds me of the age-old question: if you replace the head of an ax twice, and the handle three times, is it the same ax??

In any case, our *cabaña* turned out to be the envy of other properties along the beach due to a law that restricted the building of any new structures within sixty feet of the beach.

We loved being grandfathered.

*   *   *

Once again we heard from Hans, who invited us for lunch to introduce Tomas, his new partner on the now consolidated balance of his land to the west of us. Tomas was a smooth fellow . . . I thought arrogant. Hans had told us that he was a doctor who consulted on pandemics all around the world and who happened to think Cabarete was up and coming . . . a good place to invest his money.

Before our sandwiches arrived, the purpose of the meeting was clearly stated: *Would we like to put our property back in with theirs, along with a half million dollars, for an interest in their, as of yet, undefined venture?*

Their proposal caught us completely by surprise. In fact, we were dumbfounded. Actually, Tomas's notoriety had preceded him about a week before this meeting, but we didn't connect him to the scuttlebutt until then.

Word had it that Tomas had lent $900,000 to a contractor friend in Germany who wanted to develop the Pequeño Refugio hotel immediately east of our lot. When payback time ran out,

Tomas not only refused to extend the loan, but sent a lawyer and *Policía* . . . guns drawn . . . who entered the lobby of the hotel, told the manager that Tomas was the new owner, and that he was fired as of that moment. With the paperwork to substantiate it, as well as the guns, the manager left, *rápido*. About a one minute notice and Tomas took over as the new owner. Just like that.

Bill and I, without even discussing it, knew that Hans' proposal did not fit in our vision for our life in Cabarete; nor did the new partner interest us in the least. We did like Hans and hoped he knew what he was getting into.

It didn't take long for that "undefined venture" to become clearly defined. Tomas, between trips consulting on pandemics worldwide, continued his Cabarete epidemic. He decided to renovate Pequeño Refugio from a hotel into condos at the same time that the excavation for his project with Hans had begun on the other side of us. They had named that one *The Palace* and it filled the entire lot, leaving about 2 meters (six feet) from street to beach, and from the east and west lot lines. It was completely oversized for the building lot. Corruption, so prevalent in the Dominican Republic, governed building permits and bent any laws that existed to the person who offered the highest bribe. There was nothing we could do to stop them since the path must have been smoothed with *mucho pesos*. The Palace was ostentatious and ugly. The construction on either side of us went on for at least three years.

*   *   *

Two days before we were due to leave for home, and only a few minutes after our nightly walk on the beach where the stars were out, millions of them, and a quarter moon silvered the wave crests, Bill and I decided to eat dinner in the Windsurf restaurant before our swim. It was now dark and I dashed into the hotel bathroom to do something with my hair-gone-wild, intending to catch up with Bill in the lobby. As I hurried toward the sidewalk which bridged a drain gutter, I missed the walkway in the semi-darkness, stepped into the gutter and my full weight came down on my left ankle. I dropped to the sidewalk and almost immediately thought I was going to throw up or pass out. A kind passerby asked if he could help and I replied to please find Bill in the lobby.

Within seconds Bill was there and upon seeing my ankle, he rushed to the bar and returned with a large bucket of chipped ice, carefully plunging my foot into it. I was crying with the pain and the cold.

After a bit, the nausea passed and all I wanted to do was to go up to our apartment. Bill, with the help of a hotel guard, first tried sitting me on a plastic chair, but it was too flimsy and buckled under my weight when they picked it up. Then, I told them how to do a Red Cross carry, which I had learned from my mother when she was teaching volunteers in the 1940s.

While being transported in a Red Cross carry, the victim's head is at the same level as the two carriers, inches apart. By the time the guard and Bill had labored up the three flights with me balanced on their crossed hands, they were sweating bullets and

I was giggling almost hysterically.

Not long after Bill had set me up in the apartment with pillows and more ice, the chef, who along with everyone else in the dining room had heard the commotion, kindly sent up a marinara spaghetti dinner with my favorite garlic toast and pineapple cake for dessert.

In the morning, my ankle was hugely swollen and bright purple. I used a chair as a crutch and helped Bill pack us up for the trip home. I stayed in the room all day and night. The next morning, José arrived in his taxi. He helped Bill load me and our baggage, and when we arrived at the airport, he told us to wait. He then ran inside, returning with a wheelchair. After a big hug and promises to see us next year, he drove away, tooting his horn.

The reception desk was crowded with a large group of people pressing forward wanting to be first at the counter, as is the way of all "lines" in the DR. Much to our surprise and pleasure, one of the porters took hold of the chair handles and wheeled us right past the front of the crowd to the check-in counter, and then up to the gate for boarding. I felt like royalty, with a sympathetic husband and a throbbing foot.

When our flight was called, they even wheeled me into the plane, stopping in first class. I tried to tell them it was a mistake, but the stewardess flashed me a charming Dominican smile, pointed at my ankle which Bill had wrapped with about ten feet of ace bandage, and helped us to be seated. The flight to Newark Airport was actually enjoyable since first class was a treat for both of us, with free drinks and a good meal, complete with hot, moistened towels to wash our hands.

By the time we obtained another wheelchair in Newark, went through customs, and were wheeled to the gate for Boston, we missed our connecting flight. I felt totally bummed, but at least American Airlines did give us free hotel accommodations for the night. I was trying to be a good sport, but all I wanted was to be back home in our own bed, cuddled by Bill and surrounded by my five baby pillows.

On our way from Logan the next day, we stopped at the Portsmouth hospital for an x-ray and were told that the ankle was broken. Then, with a walking cast, as there was nothing else to do for the fracture, we finally arrived home.

Undeterred, we agreed that we couldn't wait to return to the DR.

*   *   *

Before parting with Ann and John that year, they told us that they planned to "take a break" from the DR, explaining that it wasn't only because we had essentially lost our little Casa Cabarete, or because the charm of Cabarete, for them, was buried in all the new development, but because they liked to spread their wings . . . see new places . . . have new experiences. We had suspected that this was coming, but felt enormously disappointed. Bill and I love them both, and would miss them terribly.

The Middle Lot House

The Yard Sale

Karen, ready for business

First Los Alisios Cocktail Party

NUEVE

2003 - LOS ALISIOS

Reluctantly, we had returned to New Hampshire, leaving the project in the hands of Hugh. Talk about red tape and corrupt politics . . . the DR took the cake. The way it worked, government contracts were awarded to businesses and builders in return for money paid directly to the official who made the decision. We still would not pay, and did not get the permit. With every phone call or e-mail from Hugh, we became more and more discouraged.

Bill and I returned to our Windsurf apartment No. 312 in December of 2002. Having endured delay-after-delay on building permits, and much swinging between extremes of frustration, we finally, and I do mean finally, decided to forget about constructing the three-story, 6-unit building.

One thing about me . . . I am a solution person. As soon as a problem presents itself, my mind immediately goes into overdrive to determine the best, most efficient course of action. I awakened early one morning after we had been in Cabarete about one week, and said to Bill: "This is crazy. We may be eighty in the shade before anything happens. Let's just renovate what already exists." One reason Bill and I have been such a good match is the absolute joy we both feel when either of us hits upon a great idea—and this was one of those times.

Bill sat right up. "Fantastic," he said, leaping out of bed, "let's do it." And we were off. Over breakfast, sketches were put to paper. By mid-morning some new measurements had been taken, ideas discussed, and an awful lot of excitement generated. This was going to be a blast.

Lunch with Hugh brought him on board with a willingness to do the construction calling it a *renovation*. He also agreed to use Bill's re-worked designs and expert direction, along with more than a few ideas of his own that he had to offer. Hugh said he would put an estimate together within a few days. Because it was termed simply "renovation to an existing structure" the permit could come through within a week.

Hugh explained that there is very little actual work done between Christmas and the second week of January. "This means if you are planning to do business or get something done by the government you had better get it done in mid-December, or you will be waiting until almost February." So he promised that he would start construction as soon as his crew came back from the *Navidad* celebration.

We were relieved and excited to have made a firm decision.

*   *   *

Most Dominicans are Christians and the celebration of *Navidad* is an expression of their faith. Children do not receive gifts until the Day of the Kings, which is January 5th. In fact, the government recognizes the need for gifts to be given by requiring all employers to pay their employees a double salary for the month of December. When Roque was "watchy man" for Casa Cabarete, he always greeted us upon our arrival with *Feliz Navidad?* —his hand outstretched. Which meant he expected double pay for the month. Once we understood, it became easy for us to follow the way of the DR.

In the meantime, I watched Engineer Bill refine sketch after sketch as we waited for *Navidad* to pass. We measured the existing structure in relation to the lot boundaries and proposed structure. As I held one end of the tape measure, I could envision the finished project as it took shape on paper. The way Bill and I work together on any project or adventure has always made me feel complete.

There would be about 2,200 sq. feet under roof. Bill's plan for the main part of the house was for a large open entrance to serve as Bill's Books, which would be accessible from the street and around the outside of the house from the beach. Inside, there would be two bedrooms, each with a bath, a full kitchen, and a huge dining/living room with the entire wall facing north with sliding glass doors leading to the backyard, on through a garden, to the *cabaña*, and then . . . the gorgeous beach.

In addition, we were able to create a "lockout" suite in the west end of the house with a separate entrance—one bedroom, bath, living room, and kitchenette, the ocean-side wall of sliding glass doors—privacy for future company we were pretty darn sure would be coming. And boy, did they ever. Bill even arranged for the lockout to be wheelchair accessible for my brother who stayed with us several times.

*   *   *

After spending *muchas horas* considering various name possibilities for our new property: La *Cabaña* de Playa, Mira Mar, Raya de Luna . . . we settled on **Los Alisios**, which means trade winds, the very Cabarete feature that had first brought us to the DR for windsurfing.

In front of the *cabaña*, there was a five-foot high wall separating the beach from our yard and we engaged JR, a local Dominican artist to paint our name upon it. Excited to have the job, he decided to go all out and created a colored mural of a palm tree being blown by the trade winds, along with a flow of ocean waves, to surround the scripted name: *Los Alisios*. He backed his dilapidated truck right into the yard and with his helper, hooked up a spray-gun compressor and went to work like Michelangelo. Days later, we were pleased beyond measure with his original and picturesque mural, the shades of blues and greens vibrant in the sunlight. It truly set off and identified our property for all to see as they strolled along the beach.

*   *   *

Bill's Books was still in full swing in the old house until the day before Hugh's crew was to arrive. That's when we put up signs at the street and beach entrances saying: *closed for renovation.* Hugh began as planned and very quickly the old house became unrecognizable. As he deconstructed what was there, many Dominican friends asked for and took the reusable materials: corrugated tin from the roof and all the old lumber, even if there was some rot in it. Our friend Elizabeth came after her workday with four strong men and a truck. They were thrilled to get these materials to use for their homes and we were more than happy to give it to them. As they were loading the trucks to the hilt in the dark, I commented that it was great that she had so many *caballeros* to help her, and they all burst out laughing. They interpreted my comment as *horses* which I had intended to mean *gentlemen.* Ah, Spanish, a language of many meanings.

Elizabeth invited us to her home on her day off, so Bill and I took a bus to her road and then hailed a *moto concho* for the rest of the trip. With two of us on one bike, Bill circled me with his arms, and I hung onto the driver as if my life depended on him. I knew he was laughing at me, but I didn't release my iron grip.

After a greeting of hugs and laughter, Elizabeth led us into her house that was a little bit larger than Casa Cabarete and impeccably clean. We sat at a wooden table with a cloth of orange and pink swirling design where she served us cokes and *dulce de leche* with a strong flavor of coconut in the form of candy bars. It was super sweet, but delicious. Curtains were drawn against the sun. She apologized that the cokes were warm, but that her refrigerator was, *no funciona.* Her mother and brother lived next door and came over to greet us while many children stood by eyeing the candy. Elizabeth has a beautiful smile and is very loving. She had told me that her husband *marido se quitó* and that she was happy without him.

There were freshly washed sheets draped on a fence next to a small garden with red tomatoes on the vine, onions with thick green tops, bush beans dangling among the heart-shaped leaves, cucumbers starting to vine, crisp blooms of lettuce, mangoes, and plantains which I have learned is the staple of the Dominican diet along with *arroz blanco*. I imagined that the produce was shared with her family. The sun moved across the yard and left it in afternoon shadow as we visited with some English, some Spanish and a lot of gestures.

On the way home, Bill smiled when I asked him what he thought of a refrigerator for Elizabeth. Another reason I love my husband—a generous heart.

*   *   *

After Elizabeth's daughter turned thirteen, she approached me to see if I would vouch for her to obtain a visa to the United States. She would live with an Aunt in Miami and attend public school there. I knew that visas were increasingly hard to obtain, hence the dramatic rise of illegal emigration, or the use of temporary visas to get into the States and then just overstaying the legal visit time. Our son Steve told us that more than one million Dominicans now live full or part-time in New York City and are called Dominican Yorks (your-kays). He said he had employed numerous Dominican men for construction projects and in his restaurants, and that they were good, reliable workers. He also advised that we should *not* put our names on any legal documents regarding emigration because it could come back to bite us, especially since we were trying to obtain permits from the government for construction. I felt terrible to say no to Elizabeth; however, with a little *something* from us, later that winter her daughter did make it to Miami. I love that Elizabeth wanted more for her daughter and was able to make it happen.

* * *

One early morning that was still hesitating between dawn and daylight, we were having breakfast on the No. 312 balcony. Bill observed a young man working hard on the extension to a Windsurf building. "Boy, that guy is a hustler," Bill remarked to me. And thus began our association with Aguto.

After clearing it with Hugh about having him work separately for us after he finished his present project at the Windsurf, Aguto quickly became Bill's right-hand-man around Los Alisios. I had already been scheming with gardening ideas for the yard between the house and the beach, and Bill had begun to accumulate tools for the job from the *ferretería*. The first project had to be a tool shed which they constructed against the Pequeño Refugio property-line wall.

I laughed as I watched them "talk", wave their arms, measure, and draw marks on the wall where the shed was to be located. Since Aguto spoke only Spanish and Bill only English, I decided that it would be a minor miracle if they had a meeting of minds, but I had underestimated the power of gesticulation. I realized that the language of manual labor is easy to act out when Aguto picked up a short pole and hammered it into the ground with such tenacity that there was no question as to where he thought the corner should be.

I should have remembered Bill's *tubo* adventures with Roque at Casa Cabarete, although this project would be considerably more than putting two pipes together. I decided to keep my nose out of it when Bill hopped on the back of Aguto's *moto concho*, wrapped his arms around Aguto's waist, and off they went to the *ferretería* to order supplies.

This was the first of many projects they tackled together, and I have to say that the communication they developed between them could have been a model for international relations around the world. As far as I remember, Aguto never called Bill by his name; it was always . . . *jefe,* which means boss. Perhaps the funniest episode of a linguistic breakdown was that of the telephone pole episode. When the house was near completion, we applied for telephone service at the main office in downtown Cabarete. They said we needed a telephone pole. We thought, *no problema*, since our house was only thirty feet from an existing pole on the street. But, no matter how hard Bill tried to explain with sketches and a dictionary, he got nowhere. We had to get a pole of our own . . . *privado.* It would have to be positioned on our property about six feet away from the existing pole, and would receive a wire from a transformer about 200 feet away.

Enter Aguto with a plan. He "said" he would purchase a pole in Santiago, which he could deliver in about a week. It would then be installed by him and connected up by the service people, all at a substantial cost. Don't ask me how Bill understood all of the above.

After his pole was delivered, Hugh's electrician dug a trench from the house out to where it was to be erected, and then ran wires inside the buried conduit and up to a small electric box on the wall just above ground. The telephone worker arrived the next day, reviewed the situation, and stepping carefully over our pole lying on the ground, he ran wires directly from their street pole down, inside our wall, and connected to Hugh's wires in the box.

Aguto had not appeared for several days. Bill, muttering to himself, not too softly, rolled our pole up against the front wall . . . out of the way. In the meantime, our service was on, and we made our first call. Aguto's pole rested peacefully . . . and horizontally.

When Aguto strolled into the yard the next week he and Bill had an animated discussion followed by Aguto showing up a short time later with friends and a truck. The pole disappeared. Not too upset, Bill figured it was headed for the *barrio* west of Cabarete where Aguto lived, and probably used for an extension of free power to a needy family, somewhat like what we had at Casa Cabarete.

'Tis a far better use . . ." Bill said to me, with a twinkle in his eye.

*   *   *

Along with overseeing the construction, Bill was still pursuing the sport of windsurfing. I had given up accompanying him. I just didn't have the strength to hold steady against the wind and waves, although I did still venture out on the lake in New Hampshire . . . when the conditions were just right.

One time, when I walked up the beach to meet him after his sail, Bill introduced me to Paul, a fellow windsurfer. His wife Eileen didn't sail either, so we fell into the pattern of sitting under a palm tree to watch our husbands, and to talk. About our children, of course.

Bill said that he and Paul bonded immediately, not only because they were two older guys who enjoyed windsurfing, but mainly because Paul's company in Milwaukee had designed and built the staging and acoustics for the Dominican Republic National Theater in Santiago—one similar to the Lincoln Center in New York City. I knew then that they would have a lasting friendship with that acoustical interest in common. A year later the four of us visited that theater to see and hear all about Paul's amazing project.

*   *   *

Every day while staying at the Windsurf Resort, Bill and I rushed across the street, excited that work was in progress. It was fun for me to watch as his drawings become reality; my favorite was the large-tile floors, placed on the diagonal throughout, which made the space so much more inviting when you first enter the house.

The Dominican way of construction was unique to say the least. For instance, the plasterer would create a wall and finish it with *pañetta*. Then the electrician would enter the scene, sit on his haunches, and with a hammer and chisel, chip away a vertical line in the newly plastered wall, run his conduit in the groove, and then re-*pañetta* the wall with the conduit embedded—all of which took hours, but made enjoyable by hot rhythms of Merengue blaring loudly throughout the house. The workers all talked at once among the debris and Hugh acted as the referee, while Bill's Spanish continued to be a mixture of poor grammar and builder's slang. The construction on the house progressed, sometimes with great speed, and other times slower than the slugs in the garden.

When the workers prepared for the concrete roof, we climbed the outside stairs attached to a balcony on Pequeño Refugio Hotel next door, for a bird's eye view of the process. Talk about excess . . . we never saw so many steel re-bars lying crisscrossed on top of the support beams. Literally, hundreds of them. And then, the day they "poured" the roof was fascinating. Along with Eileen and Paul, we watched the entire process and prayed that the cement block walls of Los Alisios were strong enough to hold up thousands of pounds of cement.

The pour took about three hours, as one truck after another

came down the main street, stopping all other traffic for a few minutes as they maneuvered into position. They would unload the special piece of equipment, which forced the cement up a tube to above the roof, where the lead concrete placement worker directed the slurry into the formwork. It covered the steel rods as well as the conduit for all the ceiling fans and lights yet to be installed. Between the traffic stoppages and the hustle of the workmen, I noticed people up and down the street watching the progress of the pour. They seemed almost as enthused as we were. By late afternoon the roof was done. All was quiet as the cement hardened in place. The house was gradually taking shape.

That evening, Bill and I hugged and raised a toast to the roof and the setting sun across the water. It had been an exciting day.

*   *   *

While Los Alisios was under construction, Nancy and Doug decided to visit Cabarete again and asked us to book them a room at Sans Souci, a hotel right on the water and only a block away from us at the Windsurf. After they checked in, Doug came over to ask us if they could borrow our "college" size refrigerator, an extra one that he knew we had stored in No. 312. The fridge at Sans Souci was not working.

Bill offered to help him carry it back to their place, but Doug assured us that he could handle it. Not ten minutes later the security man at the Windsurf knocked on our door and told us that he had captured the man who had stolen our refrigerator and was holding him in the lobby while waiting for the *policía*. It took some explaining, but we finally got it straightened out. The *hombre* from the *policía* then actually carried the refrigerator over, for a handsome tip, and helped Doug set it up. *No problema.*

* * *

While sitting under the thatched roof of a beach *bohia* that offered a tiny pool of shade, Nancy and I watched our husbands submerged in the ocean up to their chests as the water level rose and receded. At the same time, three young lovelies had settled themselves several hundred feet away from us, placed their towels on the sand with care, removed their suit tops and lathered their bodies, preparing for some serious tanning.

In the meantime, the boys were waiting for just the right wave to come along: one that would start to break when they pushed off the bottom, swam a few strokes, and then rode the wave to the beach. Beyond them, a riot of billowing, multicolored windsurf sails cutting in and out of one another flirted dangerously with swimmers who ventured further out from shore. I reached for my shades as the sun's white line shimmered down the water and blazed across the sand.

We noticed how Doug and Bill seemed to have gradually drifted down the beach from us, either for better rollers, or as Nancy suggested, to obtain a more advantageous landing spot and a better view of the sunbathing beauties.

A dog that had been dozing in the shade with us raised his head, looking speculatively at me. I poured some water into my cupped hand and he drank appreciatively. At Los Alisios, I had asked Aguto to create a small foot rinse basin next to the stairway from the beach to the *cabaña*. More than for that reason, I kept it filled with fresh water for all thirsty dogs passing our way.

*   *   *

My birthday comes in February, and on that day, I felt rather sick. We had plans to go out for dinner with Nancy and Doug and had invited them to first have cocktails in our *cabaña* by the sea. Sitting there waiting for them and watching the sun setting beyond the final windsurfers of the day, I was thinking of ways to graciously get out of the evening plans just as they arrived.

Walking toward us across the yard, they were followed by an entourage of waiters from the Windsurf restaurant. The lead waiters were carrying a table, four chairs, a white tablecloth, linen napkins, and candles, which they deftly set up under our *cabaña* just as the moon was rising over the water. They were quickly followed by more waiters carrying a three-course dinner. At that point in the construction of Los Alisios, there were probably fifty or more supports made of tree trunks wedged vertically between floor and the new roof forms, so the waiters had to weave their way through that unique forest. Not surprisingly, I made a sudden recovery. We all had a memorable evening while the Big Dipper hung over us; the other constellations clear as a star chart; the Milky Way like lace unfurling.

Mindful of my lament that our garden needed a white flowering plant to compliment all the colorful ones, Nancy, *who always gets thing done*, remembered seeing one sitting all by itself in the front yard of Tropicoco Restaurant. She had the chutzpah to take a cab there and convince the owner to sell it to her (who actually provided a shovel.) I can only imagine Nancy rushing back by cab, triumphant, with the plant sitting on her lap—roots, dirt, white blossoms and all.

And Doug, in addition to advising Bill on the electrical and internet layout, memorialized the entire building of Los Alisios, along with friend Hank, by photographing every step of construction right through completion and then they both presented us with a CD that to this day makes us sigh with memories.

*   *   *

Lynn, Nate, and family came bearing a gift for my birthday that completely took me by surprise. It was a quilt lovingly handmade by Bill's girls—Lynn, Cathy and Barbara, depicting the various "houses" that had played a part in my personal history. It was an amazing work of art sewn in beautiful detail that blended with our color scheme: royal blue and yellow. (Now I knew why Lynn had been so interested in what colors we had chosen for the living room furniture.) Bill hung it on the wall near the door where all could admire it each time they passed through. Especially me. I treasure it.

*   *   *

Eileen and Paul had been following the progress of Los Alisios, each day trudging down the beach from their favorite hotel, The Palm Beach Condos. We would invite them to a cold *Presidente* under the *cabaña* to hear their ideas and to discuss all kinds of possibilities. When the house was nearing completion, they offered to go with us to Santiago in our quest for furnishings. I was thankful for Eileen's help since, being an antique lover, I did not have much experience in buying *new* furniture. With the name of three stores that Socorro had given me on a slip of paper, we set out for Santiago.

For this trip, José decided to take the mountain route, which headed southward off the main highway to Santiago, a little bit west of Sosúa. Up and down, left and right, we twisted and turned over narrow roads, through small villages, past school kids walking arm and arm, and grandmothers holding babies while, perhaps, the mother was working. A long way off, there was a mutter of thunder and the brief flicker of lightening, distant and ornamental. Somebody else's storm. I held my breath many times, but José knew where he was going, driving not aggressively, just casual and efficient. Of that there was no doubt.

Something about me . . . I do not like shopping. If I need something, I just enter the appropriate store with blinders on, go directly to the item, buy it, and leave. So when José delivered us to the first store on the list, after a quick tour of their large showroom and extensive inventory, I said to my furniture committee: "This is it. We will furnish Los Alisios entirely from here." And we did.

Bill and I had no problem choosing three bedroom sets made of dark-stained rattan with matching bureaus, nightstands, mirrors, and firm mattresses. For the living room, a graceful set of two couches, two matching comfy chairs, and a coffee table, all of them a golden colored rattan.

I had noticed Paul calling Bill over to point out a rattan rocking chair with a built-in magazine slot in one arm, and glass holder in the other arm. They both tried them out, and I suspect there was some collusion about watching a future football game or a magnificent sunset in comfort. Paul strongly suggested that we should have two rockers to round out the spacious living room area, otherwise it would appear barren. We had to agree.

At this point, the owner of the store told his salesman that he would take over. He wasn't exactly wringing his hands, but we knew that ours would probably be one of their larger single sales of the month. Maybe the year. Now, with his guidance, and nudges from Eileen and Paul, we then purchased an ornately inlaid mirror from Bali, a Parson's table, and a large pine cupboard to house the television and CD player. It looked very much like an antique one we had at home.

Next came Eileen's influence . . . the color of the pillow coverings. I mentioned that the combination of blue and yellow was a favorite of mine. She proceeded to paw through numerous books and came up with several possible samples. Bill and I decided on the sky blue and daffodil-yellow striped pattern among the choices she presented. While the owner wrote up the sales slip, our former salesman arrived with a tray of complimentary Dominican coffee. How could we refuse? Too strong for me, but graciously accepted.

In our shopping exuberance we hadn't thought too much about the logistics of actually furnishing the not-quite-completed house, and when we were told that the delivery date would be in four weeks, I asked, with trepidation, if they would simply store everything for us until we returned to the DR in the coming December. The owner gave me a blank look.

"You mean to keep everything here for *seven* months?" he said incredulously. "I don't know. I just don't know."

Bill had wandered off while we were dickering. He returned now with: "Honey, come look at this elegant table Paul and I just discovered."

The owner stayed right with us. The round table was a must-have: over six-foot in diameter, a stone top nearly two inches thick, in a luscious shade of marbleized bottle green resting on a sturdy rattan base. We could just picture it along with eight chairs in our huge dining space at Los Alisios. Since my feet didn't quite touch the floor when sitting on the chairs, I asked if they would be able to add a rung between the front legs. The owner knew he had us on this sale now, and graciously said he would customize the one chair especially for me. We shook hands on it.

Choosing one of the most expensive single items in the store in addition to the rest of our order convinced the owner that, with a more than substantial deposit, he could and would be glad to store our purchases for us—the furnishings for an entire house.

José had been patiently dozing in his van while we superbly accomplished our mission. Before returning to Cabarete, he drove us to his favorite restaurant in Santiago where we had to shout over the noise of a baseball game on the TV. Nonetheless, the "committee" relished an excellent lunch with a side salad seasoned with lime, soy sauce and garlic. A meal José helped us order, as well as eat.

* * *

Doors and windows would be an important part of the completed house, and Bill was concerned with the acoustic quality due to both the noise from the street and the roar of the ocean. He visited Ocean Dream, a large project under construction by Georges, a builder who imported his doors and windows from Canada. They were top quality. That same afternoon I saw the three of them— Bill, Georges, and Hugh measuring the openings in the now nearly completed concrete structure that was to be Los Alisios. More sketches were made. It wasn't until nearly seven that evening before Bill returned to No. 312 with a triumphant smile and told me of his fantastic luck: that Georges added our order for the super acoustic quality doors and windows to his, and that they would be on his next shipment due to arrive within two weeks. That's another reason I adore Bill, he's a *solution person* too.

*   *   *

Once again, it was time for us to leave Cabarete. We packed up our belongings in No. 312, and called José for a ride to the airport. Then we dashed across the street for one final check on the soon-to-be-completed Los Alisios. As we stood in the yard on the ocean side of the house in the intense heat of the sun, I said to Hugh, "Gee, I wish we had thought of putting in a swimming pool."

He replied, "Well, this is the time to do it if you are ever going to, because we could just add it to the same permit."

Without further discussion, Bill ran across the yard, picked up the long water hose that was lying in a heap, and stretched it out on the ground in the shape of a large rectangle. "How about putting the pool there?" he asked Hugh.

"Looks good to me, and just the right size," Hugh responded, his eyes crinkling into a smile. "Good thing you mentioned it. I'll email you an estimate."

Bill paced off what he had laid out. "I'll draw up sketches for the walkways in the yard and around the pool, and the gardens. I'll fax them to you ASAP."

When José beeped the horn impatiently several times from the street, we gave Hugh a big hug and ran for the taxi—hating to leave just as Los Alisios was transforming into such an amazing place. Off we went in the early morning. New Hampshire still light-years away from thought.

Renovate Old House

The Cement Roof

J R and Ocho Painting Mural

DIEZ

2004 - SETTLING IN

Back home in New Hampshire, I spent a lot of my free time accumulating household items to take with us, anticipating our return to the hopefully completed Los Alisios in December. Towels, sheets, stainless silverware, Corelle dishes, sheer drapes for the sliding glass doors, shower curtains, and good-as-new Revere pots I found in Goodwill. And, when Bill wasn't paying attention, I was able to bury a brand new Sears's vacuum cleaner amongst towels in the bottom of a huge duffle bag I had bought at the Army-Navy store. We would be able to set up instant living once all these things found their way to Los Alisios. Bill packaged and shipped via FedEx our used hot/cold water cooler that would accommodate the five-gallon bottles that were available at Janet's *super mercado,* just a short walk up the street. He also managed to strap a small dolly to one of our suitcases so that we could use it to transport the water bottles from Janet's to Los Alisios. I was trying to think of every possible necessity as well as convenience.

Well aware that it can be difficult to acquire basic items that one may find in any US drugstore, I also stocked up on Band-Aid's, rubbing alcohol, cough syrup, cold medicines, soap, toothpaste, A&D ointment, Rolaids, peroxide, saline solution, antibiotic cream, sun lotions, Ibuprofen, aspirin. You name it, I thought of it. Here's what I had not anticipated: Los Alisios become a dispensary for all minor ailments of our Dominican friends.

*   *   *

December 2003 finally came.

A trouble-free trip until we were about to go through customs at the airport in Puerto Plata, where you have to put your bags up on a counter so the inspectors can rummage through the contents. Waiting in line, Bill suddenly became nervous thinking about all the things we were bringing into the country. So, completely unlike him, he wrapped a ten-dollar bill around the handle of each bag as he lifted it to the counter, and the inspector, with practiced sleight of hand, smoothly slid each bill into his pants pocket as he waved every bag through without another glance.

In the cab with José, who had given us a warm greeting, Bill told me *very firmly* that he would never sneak things into the DR again. I was okay with that since I couldn't think of another thing that we'd ever need that wasn't already right there in the taxi with us.

Knowing our flight schedule, Hugh was anxiously waiting for us in front of Los Alisios, eager to see our first impression. José turned into the yard and we jumped from the cab. We followed Hugh through the arched entry to the spacious foyer where, by design, Bill and Karen would be setting up Bill's Books. Hugh then opened the front door, and we gasped in unison: "Oh. My. God!"

The interior was magnificent beyond our wildest imagination . . . the diamond patterned cream-colored tile floor throughout, the soaring white ceiling in the living room, the soft yellow walls, and the expansive sliding glass doors leading out to the gardens which Aguto had not only maintained, but enhanced amazingly over the summer . . . it was a stunning sight.

I remained rooted to the spot as I tried to absorb the total impact of the vision before me. No words could describe it. Neither Hugh nor Bill uttered a sound until I recovered to the point of saying in near reverence: "Hugh, it's beautiful! I love it. Thank you, thank you." Then we crushed Hugh in a three-way hug.

Seeing the culmination of all our plans come together set up some kind of vibration between Bill and me as, hand in hand, we began touring the main house—the bedrooms and baths, the kitchen area, and then into the full lock-out suite, which also had a large sliding glass door looking out to a patio and the sparkling swimming pool. I kept stopping with each turn to throw kisses to Hugh. I'm positive our reactions were totally satisfying to him. Our praise was certainly well, well deserved. He had done a fantastic job. Bill and I could not have been happier.

I had emailed the furniture store in Santiago that we would be ready and anxious for them to deliver our furnishings the afternoon of our arrival. Bill and I were still walking through the rooms and yard like kids in a candy store when they arrived in mid-afternoon in a moving van, plus a large enclosed truck. There were four "movers" ready to unload, plus Bill and Aguto, while I stood in the doorway directing where to place everything. The last item off the truck was the round stone dining table top. Five men could barely get the top out of the truck. I couldn't imagine how they would move it across the yard, through the entry foyer, and then into the house. But obviously they had done this before. Standing it on edge, like a wheel, they rolled it over long strips of heavy foam, passing from one piece to the next, on into the house.

When one of the men asked, "*Adonde?*" I realized that wherever I said to put the table, it would be there forevermore. Bill and I shoved the base frame back and forth; trying to position it under the ceiling fan and light, yet clear of the main roof support column.

"*Aqui,*" Bill finally said with certainty.

A short while later, after a few more minor position adjustments of various items throughout the house, everything was in place. We were completely satisfied. *Presidentes* were toasted all around, and then, with sizable tips for a job well done, the moving crew departed.

Los Alisios was fully furnished and would be complete once we unpacked all the items that had sailed through customs. Not that we are obsessive, or even compulsive, but Bill and I didn't stop until every last thing was in place. I thanked Eileen silently when we arranged the pillows with various designs, but all in the same blue and yellow tones as the upholstery that she had helped me choose for the couches and chairs. It was so *House Beautiful*.

Hugh had left the *Presidentes* in the fridge, and Elizabeth, bless her heart, had prepared and left two large plates of *La Bandera*, rice and beans, fried plantain and a salad in the refrigerator. Gordon came over from the Windsurf just after the moving truck departed to add his congrats and asked if we could use his help. He didn't need a tour since he had been following the construction progress with his dad almost daily. Socorro and Sandra both came by after work with house gifts and to get a first-hand tour. We felt truly welcomed into our new home.

Only then did we go for an evening dip in the ocean just as a sliver of moon could be seen above the horizon. It was an extravagantly starry night. After rinsing off, we dropped our bathing suits and slipped into our glorious swimming pool, heated all day by the sun's rays.

From that day forward, every time I walked into Los Alisios, the view would take my breath away.

*   *   *

We settled in more each day, adjusting to the spacious house, the new furnishings, the natural flow out to the gardens. Sometimes we would just wander hand in hand, not saying more than ooh and aah in varying levels or intensities. Just a look and a knowing nod of response was all that was needed—an acknowledgement of: "Yes, that was a great idea you had." It was mutual admiration for a dream turned into reality.

The only thing missing was Ann and John. We couldn't wait for their next visit to share our Shangri-La.

Orange, yellow, red . . . Bird of Paradise stalks, lavender Passion flowers, lilies like sunshine, and fuchsia orchids alternately graced the center of our stone table thanks to the charming man who came around every Friday with armloads of fresh flowers for sale. His whistle would bring me running from the yard. I used to say that if I ever won the megabucks, I would have fresh flowers delivered to my home every week. I felt like I finally hit the jackpot.

A shout was necessary occasionally to locate one another when we had wandered off alone. If Bill didn't answer, I would most likely find him out in the gardens, pulling weeds, or stray grass shoots whose name he didn't know, but called it 'wire grass.' His nemesis. It seemed to be a single strand, a fine taproot, about the diameter of those little multi-colored telephone wires that carry conversations around the world. It grows overnight, he complained. It was a constant battle.

We had taken a chance on an all-white, plastic wicker-like set of couch, chairs, and tables with royal blue cushions for the lockout living room. It turned out to be perfect. When guests weren't staying with us, we used that room as a transition from the pool into the house. Wet suits did not bother the tiles in the least. And, when necessary, a simple wipe down did the cleaning job.

*   *   *

Like all new homes, the overlooked details and conveniences in the planning stage began to appear. I started a list of: *to get* or *to do's,* and noticed that Bill was adding items to it. This was good, because he hadn't scratched out any of my items. It's funny how the list grew without particular comment between us. I anxiously waited to see what might be the first thing to be undertaken, completed, and lined out.

It turned out to be one of his items—a refuse and trashcan hideaway that would allow us to stow out of sight, garden trimmings, plastic kitchen bags, and general garbage. He had a brief chat with Aguto one day and within a few hours, *cemento y bloques* appeared in the yard, and a neat little barrier wall was built. Spit-spot—painted to match the wall, and off the list.

A few days later, we learned from Socorro that our water cooler had landed and we went to the customs office to pick it up. In Spanish/English and gestures, they told us that there would be an import duty charge of $140 US (not pesos.) I protested strongly, telling them that it was used and not worth much. They responded that they would keep the cooler until we produced a bill of sale. I returned the next day with a receipt from Poland Springs I had contrived on my computer, and retrieved the cooler with no import fee. I wasn't exactly proud of what I did, but felt there was no way to argue with them, and the $140 fee would have been more than our original cost. I promised myself to make up for my ruse in other ways.

At last, our computers were connected to the Internet. It was before Wi-Fi existed everywhere in Cabarete, but Hugh had kindly run wiring for Internet throughout the house, and then had installed a connecting wire from pole to pole above the street over to the Windsurf Resort. It was a big plus for us, and certainly aided our full-time living in the DR. Email and banking were now a piece of cake.

Next on the construction list were iron fences and gates to clearly delineate as well as secure Los Alisios. Hugh told us about Hernando, the "maestro of ironworks" who lived and worked in the *barrio* on the outskirts of Cabarete. José knew him by reputation, said he was *muy bueno*, and gladly drove us to his place of business. Hernando's shop was situated under a large roofed area with open sides in lieu of ventilation fans. Soot-covered antiquated forge equipment stood alongside three or four welding machines. Heavy steel workbenches with numerous random size iron vices were placed helter-skelter about the shop.

A large gazebo, probably to be located in someone's garden, was in a state of near completion in the yard. His workers on break were lounging around on the rusted appliances, car parts, and corrugated tin piles in the yard. The pungent smell of burning garbage from behind his shop mingled with the residual welding fumes.

I could tell immediately that Hernando, a large forceful man, knew his trade well and was all business. When Bill briefly explained with a flurry of pantomime what we wanted, he said he would come back with us to assess what was needed. On the way, he asked José to pass by some of his work. Every example we saw looked effective and decorative at the same time.

At the house, he kept nodding as we toured him around the property with a lot of "hand" descriptions and gestures. When he pulled out a piece of paper, I thought it was to take notes and measurements, but instead, he hesitated a moment, scratched his head, then wrote a number on the paper and handed it to Bill . . . $35,000 pesos. Bill, who had a pretty good handle on all that might be involved, gave him a quick thumbs up and they shook hands.

Hernando said, "*Mañana.*" Then he got back in José's taxi and left without another comment. We had come to learn that *Mañana*, like *una momento*, had a flexible meaning which could mean soon or two weeks from now.

Amazingly, the next morning he came with his truck loaded with some raw stock, a portable welding machine, two helpers, and then began measuring the openings to be gated. It was exciting to see such rapid progress. Bill, in his usual manner, grabbed a pad and pencil to make sketches of his vision.

Hernando watched closely, nodding comprehension and approval and then Bill dashed in the house to make a copy for each to have. Hernando added some dimensions that must have had meaning to him and his men.

There were to be rolling gates for the street and beach wall openings; each about twelve feet wide. A double swinging gate for the main entrance to Bill's Books, and then, four single gates for the passageways at each side of the house rounded it out. All would be made to suit the existing openings. At the last minute, we added to our request a circular staircase up to the roof where the broad sweep of the Atlantic Ocean could be seen from the protective reef of the bay to the far point of land about two miles away. When Hernando finished it, the staircase curved gracefully up and away like a swan's neck. A place where we could watch the fleeting brilliance of the golden hour of sunset, like the last chord of a haunting melody.

The installations began the next week and were completed within a few days. Bill obtained padlocks at the *Ferreteria*. We were secure. Hernando was indeed a master of his trade.

*　　*　　*

Visitors were more than welcome and happily, Ann and John were the first to come. By staying with us they could save their Time Share weeks at the Windsurf, to exchange for trips within the States to visit children, etc. One of our favorite things to do together was to walk the beach, joining a stream of hungry patrons reviewing menus posted in front of numerous restaurants just as the blanching heat of the day receded. We got into the scene with the colorful fairy lights strung between slender palms that cut outlines against the sky and haunting strains of music thrumming in the background. Our choice was often influenced by a charming hostess standing on the beach, like the goddess, Circes, luring us to choose their restaurant's fare.

Bill, assuming the role of social director, decided that we should have a proper Los Alisios house-warming party as well as celebrating the arrival of Ann and John. I agreed and made arrangements with Ramón to cater it. He was the former manager of the Windsurf restaurant, and currently had his own café directly across the street from us. One item we kiddingly put on our list was a zip-line from our rooftop, over the road, ending at our favorite table in his café. That item never did get done.

We invited new and old friends, many of whom had attended our initial dilapidated-house-buying celebration two years before. The list was extensive as we realized that we had been coming to the DR off and on for over fifteen years. We loved what Hugh had created and were truly proud.

Everyone laughed, drank margaritas, Presidentes and all kinds of rum concoctions while feasting from platters of fresh pineapple, kiwi, melons, guacamole, and a variety of cheeses.

Among the attendees in addition to Ann and John: Gordon and Bego with their new baby Kai, Gordon's mother and husband, Ana and family, Sandra and Carole, Ian and Lynn, Nancy and Doug, Eileen and Paul, Doug and Marguerite, Karen and Richard, Elizabeth and Socorro came over from the Windsurf during break from work . . . and so many more. Especially Hugh, who proudly and justifiably, took credit for his work. Over thirty guests arrived at five pm and their exclamations of appreciation delighted us as we toured everyone through our fabulous Dominican home.

An additional benefit gained from the party was to show off the enhanced quarters for Bill's Books. While it had been closed for renovations, Bill and Karen had contracted to have three sets of clam-shell-like bookcase cabinets made which could be moved around on casters then folded closed and locked tight when the store was closed; thus keeping the books both safe and relatively clean. It was a great system. During Los Alisios construction, the cases had been moved to a temporary downtown quarters in José O'Shay's restaurant entranceway. Now, they were set up attractively, as planned, in our foyer leading to the front door of the house.

Karen proudly informed everyone who would listen that Bill's Books was noted in the *Lonely Planet* travel book. Excitedly, I looked it up in the most recent edition only to find that they had listed Bill's Books under . . .*where to find Beach Trash!* Oh well, Karen told me that she saw many vacationers with the Lonely

Planet book in hand when they arrived at the store.

Bill let it be known that in addition to Karen's set hours after she finished teaching for the day, the store would be open anytime he put the sign out. I laughed as I knew he loved to chat with customers and would probably have that sign out most of the time.

Now that we were ecstatically ensconced in Los Alisios, Bill put up a rental notice in Bill's Books for our apartment No. 312 at the Windsurf Resort. Living directly across the street, we were able to oversee any rentals that we set up. Two weeks or two days, we didn't care; it was just good to use the space—the sixteen weeks a year for forty years. We should live so long.

* * *

A funny thing in Cabarete (and probably everywhere else in the world) when someone is explaining where a place is, they often start out with . . . "Well, do you remember where Mario's Restaurant used to be . . . ?" This is not uncommon since there is a tremendous amount of turnover with businesses started along the street and especially on the beach, with high hopes and a shoestring, struggling to stay alive. Every year we encountered new restaurants, so it was natural and fun to try out each one as soon as possible.

Just a three-minute walk from Los Alisios, *Ocean Taste* had opened while we were away—you know, where Mariposa used to be.

Bill and I, of course, went there for lunch and were greeted by the owner, René, a most charming and dedicated restaurateur who had previously been in business in Santiago. Looking around at his patrons, we saw satisfaction everywhere. The décor, the food, the chef, and the waiters, everything was well done, and we told him so. There was only one flaw that jumped out at us—the menu.

Unable to *not* say anything about the menu, which was an eight-pager, presented in French, German, Spanish, and English, as politely as possible, we asked him if he would like us to take one home to review for *typos*? It would be good for the Americans and Canadians, I added.

"Yes, that would be a big help for me," he replied, and handed Bill a full menu to go.

I was thankful that he understood the word typo since I never could have explained it in Spanish.

Walking the beach back to Los Alisios, we couldn't help but laugh. Oh, my, what a lot of typos. I immediately thought of Liz, my dear friend and fellow writer, also the former Poet Laureate of Portsmouth, who was due to arrive the next day. Maybe she would take a shot at it.

After some good beach time and adjustment to the Dominican lifestyle, Liz did indeed jump into the project, creating whole new pages with corrected descriptions, spelling, and punctuation. The three of us really got into devising ways to describe items such:

the pallet would quiver in anticipation of the dish to be presented on the table.

After four days, Liz thought the project was done. "Except," she said, "what on earth is a drink called . . . *Aunt Mary*? The spelling was right, but I just have never heard of it."

We were stumped, until Bill suddenly said: "Hey, that's a direct translation from Spanish to English of the liquor, *Tía María*." The three of us nearly rolled on the floor, hysterical.

The next day, we delivered the final version to René, who went over it carefully, and then presented the three of us with a special card: *Regular customer 20% discount.*

"The first of its kind," Rene told us proudly. As it turned out, well worth it, Liz said, and we agreed.

* * *

The munificence of Los Alisios assailed me with each new day— how utterly thrilled I was with the way it turned out . . . a place where I could have a perpetual honeymoon with my amazing husband. A honeymoon we didn't have nearly thirty years before, since we were both working and only able to take a long weekend to celebrate our marriage. We spent the ensuing years "growing up" our kids and launching them, and building our businesses to the point of retirement.

February of 2004 I would turn seventy, so you can understand how happy I was to learn that my children and their families had planned a celebration in Cabarete. Although they had already visited us at the Windsurf, I was excited to have them all here *at the same time* and of course, for them to see, in person, our exquisite home on the beach.

Arriving on different flights, José made several trips to the airport ferrying the families to Los Alisios. It was thrilling to see their expressions as each came through the door and then again as we toured them around the house, through the lock-out, past the pool, up onto the roof deck for views all the way to Bozo Beach and out to the breakwater. Then we guided them through the gardens to the *cabaña*, and finally out to the beach. By the third telling, Bill said he felt like a tour guide but he would gladly do it over and over, if asked.

Anticipating eleven of us in the house for the ten days, we borrowed two cots from the Windsurf Resort in addition to the three blow-up mattresses we had acquired over the years. The refrigerator and pantry were loaded with food, and Ramón had been placed on alert should we call for dinners that could be sent over from his café across the street, which we did on more than one occasion.

And my birthday celebration week began.

For breakfast, the whole gang frequented René's Ocean Taste where granddaughter Roshana always chose their French toast, slathered in fresh fruit. Out in the open, the chef had a complete kitchen set-up where one could watch as he chopped vegetables, vibrant mauve onions, burgundy eggplants, and ripe avocado.

The minute he spotted Roshana coming down the beach, he'd wave to her and start preparing her favorite. The outdoor portion of the restaurant was a large patio-like terrace that bordered the beach, with a low wall of coral stone that was raised about two feet above the sand. We sat at tables pushed together on the terrace, easily accessible to beach vendors. They'd place their tray of goods on the wall for the diners to peruse. Roshana and Talia had such fun bargaining with them for a necklace or a bracelet. Roshana told me recently that she still wears hers. By unspoken agreement with all restaurants on the beach, vendors would leave without complaint as soon as the food was served.

Instantly, fresh squeezed orange juice and a dish of fragrant sections of lime were placed in front of us, while waiters jotted down our individual orders. Early morning, and already heat rose from the beach in a wavering blur. Being there with my family, the sun felt like an embrace, and I took many pictures, held for posterity by my trusted Canon camera. As we ate the unending supply of French toast or *huevos*—scrambled, fried, or once over lightly garnished with fresh tarragon—there was always a beach dog sitting just beyond the wall, patient and unblinking, watching every mouthful with underprivileged expressions. They were never disappointed.

Roshana and Talia adopted a cat that hung out at René's. It lay sprawled in the sun among the fuchsia petals of a bougainvillea vine that were scattered like confetti on the tiled terrace. My sweet granddaughters made me promise to give him lots of loving after they went home. Not a difficult task for me.

*   *   *

Julie B. and Shary performed miracles in our little kitchen, whipping up sumptuous lunches and concocting yummy hors d'oeuvres for our late afternoon gatherings. They tried to surprise me with my mother's coffee cake, but my mouth watered knowingly as the scent of cinnamon wafted throughout the house.

My birthday event became like pollen attracting bees from all over the world. Cousin Evan appeared out of the blue, and Ari's brother, Hudi flew in, detouring from Miami for a few days while on his way back to his home country, Israel. We loved having him with us. He added a spark to any family gathering. Bobby, from Portsmouth, had joined with Shary for the birthday assembly. He proudly wears his Native American heritage. Neither he nor Hudi had met before, nor had they ever been to Cabarete.

The second morning, Hudi awoke early and decided to take a walk on the beach to see what was around the northeast bend in the shoreline. "Bobby, want to go with me?" I heard Hudi ask, and on the spur of the moment, they left.

They were gone most of the day. Although they were "big boys," we anxiously started looking for them by midafternoon and were greatly relieved when they casually strolled down the beach, through the *cabaña*, and dove into the pool.

We all gathered around and listened to the following account, given by Bobby and punctuated occasionally with details by Hudi, of their adventure in the wilds of the DR:

"While casually strolling and spuriously scanning the beach for shells, we soon arrived at the targeted bend, where the breakwater met the shore. An extremely wide beach spread out before us. It was relatively empty, except for a couple of people on horseback leaving a rustic stable nested among the trees. Even though neither Hudi nor I *habla'd* Espanola, nor did the manager of the stables speak English, we were able to hire two horses and followed the guide through many puddles on a narrow dirt road shaded by trees.

Before I knew it, we were on the other side of a small town. There was a little dock and a bar along the 'Rio Sabañeta de Yasica.' We tied the horses in a grove and ordered a beer, just as a boat appeared—a metal rectangular one with three benches across the width. It had a small outboard. We decided a little boat trip was in order. Saying adios to our horses and guide, who said he would wait, we headed further inland on the river that wound its way through marshy banks.

As the reedy part of the river faded, there were a few posh abodes along the bank delineated by stonewalls. I believe we even passed a golf course. Continuing, we crossed under a major road and almost immediately pulled up to a dock in front of a resort. There was an impressive courtyard with about fifteen tables spread out among various vegetations.

While we waited for our beer, we noticed there were these

walled-in boxes along the path from the docks to the courtyard that looked like huge planters. Hudi, curious, looked in one and suddenly leaped back . . . three feet in the air! Inside was a huge snake, a python. Those "planters" were actually cages, but the tops were completely open—no screen or anything. Hudi had an extreme aversion to snakes, so jumped back into the boat, anxious to leave.

The trip back to our horses seemed quicker. At the beach, we ran them along the shore and then in the water through the waves. We only paused once, to collect the stirrup that had broken off my saddle, because I had been standing on it, kind of like a jockey.

The guide then made us stop at the breakwater. We tried, but couldn't convince him to let us ride all the way back to Los Alisios. We had very much wanted to suddenly appear at the *cabaña* on horseback. After a short walk we arrived back at Los Alisios."

No one spoke at the end of Bobby's tale until Shary broke the silence: "An epic adventure," she declared. "All in one day. Surreal. A metaphor for life."

* * *

Grandson Elan, full of energy as a teenager, raced on the beach and endlessly played in the surf. He initiated a game of Ultimate Frisbee and everyone played it right in front of Los Alisios. The rule was, you could only take three steps when you caught the

Frisbee and then had to flip it to one of your teammates until one of them reached the endzone to score the point. Two French children staying at Pequeño Refugio Hotel next door wanted to play and to my amazement, Elan was able to explain the rules well enough for them to join in the fun. One shoeshine boy dropped his box when Elan beckoned to him, picking up the idea instantly, and a little girl joined in, no more than seven or eight, who had been selling homemade *dulce con leche* on the beach. Talia was the up and coming star of Frisbee. Ari and Stevie played with them until exhausted. Bill and I had very short times on the field of play.

*   *   *

The DR is one of the biggest cigar producers in the world; they are for sale around every corner, both good and bad quality, often at disproportionate prices. We learned that most cigars from the Cuevas Hermanos factory are bought by famous brands and resold under their labels. Hugh, who enjoyed an occasional cigar, made me laugh at the image he described of a puffing machine in the factory, which sent a measured blast of air through each cigar to ensure a good draw.

One late afternoon, the wind picked up and leaned into the high palm fronds that swayed widely on their slender trunks. The sky had gone from blue to gray to black. Bill, Bobby, Ari, and Stevie made a mad dash to the *cabaña*. There was a sudden shift in the texture of the air, it was close and humid. A heavy rain began to spill down on the cement roof sounding almost like hail. Bobby had purchased cigars from a convincing beach vendor and under the protection of the *cabaña,* they all lit up.

The wind driven rain was blowing a slight mist on them. We girls heard Bobby yelling into the storm, like Lieutenant Dan on the shrimp boat, he told us later. He said that he was trying to figure out life's mysteries.

*   *   *

Body surfing became an exuberant daily activity for the family, who were mostly "lake people." The boys, especially, ran into the surf again and again, hurled themselves headfirst down the churning wave, then surfaced, staggered against one another, sandy foam streaming down their backs and legs, wet hair plastered in dark clumps over their brows and ears. I loved to watch them plunge into the sea as the sunlight splintered into sharp points of brightness on the tops of the waves that rolled in. Beyond them, a forest of windsurf masts swayed in the distant, shimmering blue.

Stevie and Roshana started an imaginative sand sculpture on the beach. Eventually, everyone got involved by adding intricate towers, moats, seashell paths. The next morning, as dawn was breaking, I sat beneath our *cabaña* with my first cup of coffee. The stars were fading. Only Venus was left in the sky. Just as the first purple blade of sunrise began, Roshana came quietly across the path to nestle against me. "What happened to my castle," she asked tearfully.

"Gone with the tide, my darling girl."

*   *   *

Bill had made reservations at The Castle Club for the actual birthday celebration, where Marguerite and Doug gave us an evening all to ourselves. Once again, it was absolutely charming. We were all milling around, enjoying Doug's unique architecture and artwork when Talia called to everyone to see something unusual by the pool. There on the surface, visible above the underwater lights, a cluster of 50 or more water bugs appeared to be swimming in a counterclockwise circle. Shary said they were doing an Esther Williams coordinated aquatic ballet. Bill, of course, explained that the 'bug ballet' was due to an underwater circulator return port, which created the swirling vortex. But science aside, the discovery of such a phenomenon added greatly to the enchantment for one little ten-year-old girl at her Grammie's special birthday party.

Before dinner, Stevie called us all together to sit around the living room. He then presented me with an album that he and his sisters had assembled depicting my life, with messages and nuances of love through photographs and haikus written by family and close friends. I held it against my heart and thanked them. Then they said: "read them all out loud." That was the undoing of me. I read and cried, read and cried. Marguerite brought a box of Kleenex and by the time I read halfway through, there was a pile of soggy tissues heaped next to my chair. Every entry triggered a memory of when my children were growing up in Natick, Massachusetts, and later, after Bill came into our lives. I suddenly wished that *every* family member, my brother and sister, and especially Bill's children, as well as friends, were right there in The Castle with us.

Knowing that I can so easily become tongue-tied, I had prepared the following words to read at the dinner table:

"I am so happy that we are all here together and I'd like to tell you why I feel like a woman blessed:

"—Because of my dearest husband, the man who brought joy and substance into my life, who helped me to believe in myself, who comforted me in the loss of my beloved parents and who offered a path and led the way to all kinds of adventures, everlasting respect and love, and much laughter.

"—Because of my dearest children, who drew me into motherhood and challenged me to guide us as a family, who gave me incentive to try again and again each time I stumbled, who swell my heart with abiding love, and from whom I am now learning to uplift my spirit and live in a state of grace.

"—Because of my dearest grandchildren of whom I am so proud and ever in awe, who have given me the opportunity to

just love and enjoy them, without worrying about bringing them up . . . their parents are doing a fine job of that.

"I want to raise my glass to the future of this unique, only slightly dysfunctional, and most wonderful family, to those who are here and those who are not here tonight:

"May it be good health for each one of you—may you love and be loved—may you have success in all your endeavors—may you always feel kindness toward one another—may you have peace in your hearts.

"And don't ever forget . . . a mother's love never ends."

* * *

Family and friends scattered back to their realities as Bill and I resumed our day-to-day life in Cabarete. We read and wrote as we explored our new way of life.

End of Day in Cabarete

Combs of unripe green bananas hang
heavy in the cooling scent of salt air.
I see the brilliance of sunset in the branches
of the Frangipani Rubra tree, ever in bloom.
The copper sun nudges the horizon,
undecided for a moment, then
plunges into the indescribable
blue that contains all things.
The first star trembles in the sky.

The friends we made in the DR had become important to Bill and me. We really wanted to "give back" in some meaningful way. So through the ensuing years, acting like sponsors, we took on Ana and her family who had remained settled in Casa Cabarete.

Our times at the Windsurf Apart, and then the Windsurf Resort under Gordon's management, had been full and memorable. During those vacations, we had occasionally walked up to Casa Cabarete to say hello, just to see how things were going, but that was about the extent of our involvement.

Ana's first request had come through her brother Borys, stating that she would like to build a small *colmado* in front of the house, where she could sell miscellaneous goods. Ann and John agreed that it was a good idea. Sure enough, the next year we were in town, the former front yard was in business.

A few years later, it was converted into a *restaurante* where Ana had set up tables for breakfast, lunch, and dinner. As is the case so often with a new business, her family and friends were the best customers. The kitchen was established in the space between the store and the house. A lot happening on such a little plot of land.

After Ana's youngest son Danny married Kelin, and Thania was born, he asked for permission to build a family quarter in the yard behind the house. You guessed it, Bill loves to draw plans. Danny lined up some contractor friends and they moved into their tiny "apartment" before Tommy, their second child, was born. And then several years later, Erick came along. Jimmy and

Viannely remained in the main house with Ana.

The Sunday before we left for New Hampshire that year of my birthday, Danny and family came to visit us at Los Alisios. They had just come from church, Danny in freshly pressed pants and white dress shirt, Kelin in a demure flowered dress, and Thania looking like a doll in a lacy pink party dress. They wanted Bill to be her Godfather. Sentimental Bill got teary.

It was an interesting ceremony in the small stone church just down the road from us. The ceiling was painted salmon pink like a tropical sunrise and had a profusion of Madonnas watching over us. The minister cautioned Danny and Kelin on the perils and pleasure of parenthood. Afterwards, we attended a party celebration. What a lovely family.

* * *

Someday, perhaps we four adventurers of 1987 might reinstate our original dreams and plans for Casa Cabarete, however each time we discussed it with Ann and John, the subject gained no traction and we agreed that maybe a higher purpose was being served.

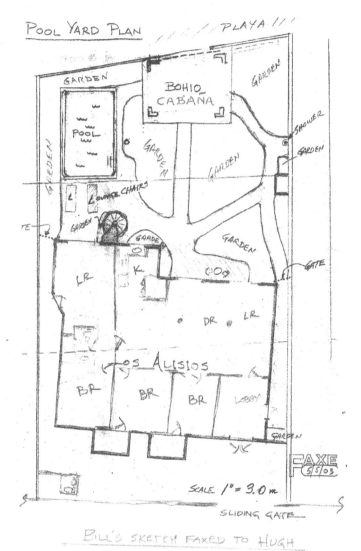

Sketch to Hugh For Yard Layout

Gate at Street

Hugh at the Pool

ONCE

2005 - SECURITY CONCERNS

The major east-west highway on the north coast of the DR splits downtown Cabarete in two. It is flanked by a tranquil lagoon on the south side and the splendid beach on the north side. Over time, Bill and I have witnessed Cabarete's conversion from a fishing village to a destination resort. I am amazed by the transformation—now there were dozens of stores and restaurants, which created an extremely congested town center.

For as long as we had been going to the DR, rumor had it that a new road was to be built around the center of Cabarete as the main route, so that the existing road could be dedicated strictly to local traffic, deliveries, and pedestrians. Considering it such an excellent idea to reduce congestion and increase business, Gordon told us that he and many other hotel and business owners in downtown contributed a great deal of money to the effort, most of which, he said, had disappeared into the pockets of Santo Domingo *politicos* . . . so much for caring about increasing trade for the locals. That obviously didn't concern them. Unfortunately, in the DR, many people aspired to elected government positions in order to be eligible for bribes. And each time government salaries were cut, the corruption grew worse. We were aware of it to some degree during the construction of Los Alisios when Hugh informed us of a variety of permits that had to be paid . . . under the table.

*   *   *

While the renewed Cabarete catered mainly to the young, sports-minded crowd, it was also perfect for those, like us, who just wanted the leisure of relaxed living, beaching, and frequent casual dining. Each morning, I could hear the scratching of rakes on the sand as young boys prepped the beach for a new day of sunbathers. They would set up rows and rows of lounge chairs; each hotel's chairs distinguished by their own bright color.

By day, local artists, souvenir shops, restaurants, supermarkets, bars, and of course, shops catering to water sports opened their doors to the beach and the main street to draw in tourists. A constant flow of foot traffic was what they all strived to attract.

At dusk, hardly skipping a beat, Cabarete caught its second wind. Restaurants and clubs flipped their attention 180 degrees by spreading hundreds of candle-lit tables and chairs on the beach hoping to lure tourists and locals for a picturesque international cuisine—a clever way to expand their seating capacity two and three fold. Waiters and waitresses balancing trays laden with drinks or meals, traipsed across the sand with ease, readily avoiding afternoon sand castles or forgotten beach toys.

Bill and I loved the whole evening experience of strolling on the beach under the stars from one place to another, choosing the restaurant for the evening . . . it was magical. As soon as we were seated, I would kick off my sandals and bury my feet in the sand. Musicians, earning their living, roamed from restaurant to restaurant to serenade both under roof and on the beach. There was one particular guitarist calling himself *Romantica* that we were fond of. The minute he'd spot us, he would come right over and stand by our table strumming and singing his heart out. Sentimental us, soon with tears in our eyes.

Long after dinner, the beach turned into a mile and half of legendary Cabarete nightlife where young vacationers and Dominicans alike partied and danced to the beat of Caribbean Latin music. One night, we bumped into the salesman who had sold us our house furniture who had come all the way from Santiago just to participate in the revelry.

"It's the absolute greatest party beach on the north shore," he told us.

Los Alisios was over a quarter mile east of the nighttime assemblage. When sitting in our *cabaña*, we could still hear the beat of electronic music, and on Saturdays at midnight, we watched spectacular fireworks, the sulfur smell mingling with the ocean salt.

Bill took credit for planning the location of our house on the lot, set back just far enough to block the late nighttime beach festivities. So just before we slept, there would only be the soothing sound of waves.

My acoustical engineer. Mr. Sound Control. My love.

*   *   *

Sandra, the Social Director at the Windsurf, whose birthday was close to Valentine's Day, invited us to join her for a celebration party at the La Roca restaurant in Sosúa. A long table was set up on the open porch, looking festive with flamboyant bouquets of scarlet bougainvillea and several bottles of champagne ready to accommodate about twenty of Sandra's well-wishers. I only recognized a few faces when we first arrived, and was pleased when Doug and Marguerite, of The Castle Club fame, hailed us to sit by them. Once we were all assembled, Sandra, wearing red, heart-shaped earrings, stood up to introduce everyone. I, being me, didn't retain many names because I don't always listen closely, but Bill, being Bill, had most of the names down pat halfway through the meal. All in all it was a vibrant, friendly, chatty group.

Periodically, people were toasting Sandra, while conversations picked up in volume, competing with general city sounds and the *moto conchos* and *guaguas* that zoomed past the porch spewing black exhaust. There was also a loudspeaker near our table that sent out waves of Merengue, with its African tom-tom beat.

We were seated directly across from a couple from New York— Cheryl and Dan with their little doggie Lolita who was peeking out of her cozy picnic basket that sat safely between them. Marguerite introduced us to them as "her new friends" from New

Hampshire. By the end of the dinner, Cheryl had invited us to join the Atlantic Book Club that met once a month in a private room right there at La Roca. She told us that over the summer she compiles a reading list for the upcoming season consisting of titles recommended by each member. She'd then email it out by October in anticipation of winter meetings in Cabarete. The person who chose a certain book would lead that discussion. Bill and I loved the idea and were quick to accept her invitation, knowing that we would appreciate the camaraderie.

There was another friend of Sandra's that we met that evening, Edith, a fascinating woman. She told us about her parents who had moved to Sosúa in 1938 when the Nazis were still allowing some Jews to emigrate. Following the Evian Conference organized in 1938 by Franklin D. Roosevelt, where delegates from 32 countries met to discuss the refugee crisis, one nation—the Dominican Republic—offered a haven, half-a-world away. Regardless of Dominican President Rafael Trujillo's self-interested motivations— large amounts of incentive money from other countries as well as from the immigrants themselves—the offer was extended and gratefully accepted. Later, I read that such journeys had become almost impossible due to the war developments, when German U-boats torpedoed the boats transporting refugees. To me, Roosevelt's decision to refuse political asylum to Jewish refugees, for whatever reason, was a shameful period in American history.

Trujillo had total control and power as a repressive dictator of the DR for a period of thirty years, ending in 1961 when his motorcade was ambushed and he was killed. The anniversary of his death is a public holiday in the DR. Although his rule brought the country more stability and prosperity, the price was high; civil liberties were nonexistent and human rights violations were routine. It is said that he was responsible for more than 50,000 deaths, all in the name of reform, and that much of his country's wealth wound up in the hands of his family and close associates.

With tears in her eyes, Edith said that her parents were forced to make the terrible choice of leaving home for a strange place they had never seen other than on a map. But, as refugees, they embarked on a journey that involved weeks of rough conditions, to a land where anti-Semitism did not exist.

Although Trujillo authorized five thousand visas, only five to six hundred Jews actually made their way to Sosúa. These settlers, who fled for their lives from Nazi persecution, were greeted by lush, tropical vegetation and welcoming people. But, as middle-class, urban Europeans, they faced frightening problems: they had to learn a new language, acquire new skills, and adjust to a new climate—all this, while worrying about loved ones left behind in Europe.

Once in Sosúa, Edith told us that her father, and every other Jewish settler, was given eighty acres of land along the coastal region, between Sosúa and Sabañeta, one cow, a horse, or a mule. With the help of their new Dominican neighbors who were friendly and willing, they began to cultivate the land, a daunting task, since they had little or no experience as to how to grow crops. She said that her father helped build the Jewish community with a synagogue and a school, conducted in Spanish, where their children and local children studied together. Those settlers ran small businesses and a thriving dairy industry, working side by side with native Dominicans.

While most of the Jews left Sosúa after the war to rebuild their lives in the United States or Israel, some families, like her own, stayed in the DR where they had become free citizens in a new country.

"Those original Jewish pioneer families who did remain in Sosúa and held onto their land, or acquired more, have made a fortune," Edith concluded, smiling broadly. "Be sure to visit our synagogue and museum while you are here."

Of course we did go to the museum, the very next day, and were filled with a sense of pride because we saw it as a testimony to the resilience of the Sosúa Jews and of humanity.

Thinking back on Sandra's party, Bill and I agreed that, not only had we had a delightful afternoon, but we had made friends with more of the interesting people who chose the DR as their home-away-from-home.

*   *   *

Cheryl was the force behind The Atlantic Book Club. She drove it, and the rest of the members enjoyed the ride. She let us all know the schedule, location, and selected book by email. For the rest of that first winter, we met in a back room at La Roca or at Cheryl and Dan's grand home in Seahorse Ranch, an exclusive community between Sosúa and Puerto Plata where they spent the winter season. Lolita, sometimes wearing cute little red bows, greeted us at the door with a friendly bark. She probably didn't weigh more than a minute.

There'd be cocktails, dinner, and a sometimes heated discussion of the book of the month—a free exchange of opinions and observations about the author, the story line, and each person's take on the message the story had to offer. Both Bill and I were pleased to partake and delighted in the intellectual stimulation.

Once Los Alisios was completed, we held several meetings there, all sitting around the huge stone table . . . perfectly suited for an intimate discussion. Margaritas were the drink of choice, and I guess the formula Bill used was pretty good, as there were no fresh limes, tequila, or triple sec left over at the end of the evening. I can still see ten frosty stem-glasses lined up with salt edging the rims as he poured his mixture.

Our house was convenient for Karen and Richard ,who were only a few miles away, Doug and Marguerite, who lived six miles east, and Dan and Cheryl who lived six miles west. Sometimes there were as many as ten of us. Bill, my social animal, loved hosting.

At one point, Global Warming became the subject *du jour*. Bill suggested the book, *State of Fear,* by Michael Crichton, for the next selection. He was sure it would bring on a lively discussion. When Cheryl agreed, he produced and handed out six copies that he had accumulated through Bill's Books. He told me that when one came in over the past few weeks, he hid it from Karen because she didn't keep duplicates in stock due to the lack of space.

Karen had smiled at me behind her boss' back.

Well, it did bring on a vigorous exchange. Dan brought in a Life Magazine from the early nineties which contained all sorts of technical data and charts proving the Global Warming trend beyond any doubt. Someone else brought in a Life magazine from the 1970s with a cover entitled Global Cooling. Others brought in articles countering every claim. Maybe we can thank the margaritas for forging a liaison of the group and overriding the somewhat contentious subject.

Bill said to me later: "See, I told you it would ignite a lively discussion."

*   *   *

A disturbing rash of robberies—perhaps due to the sinking economy and ubiquitous poverty—swept through Cabarete, setting everyone on edge and bringing unwelcome changes to our world.

Sandra, upon returning home from work, was surprised by two intruders who tied her up and locked her in the bathroom, after which they leisurely combed through her entire apartment for jewelry, cash, and anything else they thought had value. Immediately following, she and her roommate moved closer to Cabarete and at the same time had to relocate the pet donkey she had adopted. After that, they started talking seriously about returning to Canada for good. Bill and I were horrified by what happened to Sandra. A feeling of unease settled in the back of my mind.

And then, one afternoon while we were sitting on the back patio just outside the sliding glass doors of Los Alisios, a robber apparently had entered through the lockout door, and taken my sister-in-law's gold bracelets and my computer. Upon discovery, Medi cried and I fell apart since along with the computer went the manuscript for my latest novel. For some unknown reason, we did find the computer under a bush in the front yard. We surmised that the thief thought he might be too conspicuous carrying it on the street in broad daylight, and so hid it, to be retrieved after dark. Sadly, we never recovered the bracelets.

*   *   *

Upon returning to the States, I bought several thumb drives in Radio Shack to save my writings on, and a motion detector alarm to take with us on our next trip. Bill unpacked the alarm and figured out how it worked. He seemed to be okay with it. About four weeks later, a rather large box arrived by FedEx. "What the heck could this be," he asked.

"Four more motion detectors," I answered. "After everything that's been going on in Cabarete, I'm feeling uneasy about going back there."

I stared at his back, but he didn't respond.

"Okay," he said, slowly turning around to look at me, "but

aren't five motion detectors for 2,500 square feet of living space a little overkill?"

That word . . . over*kill* . . . ended the discussion.

When we returned to Los Alisios, we placed the detectors strategically around the house. Each one had its own separate remote, so our routine of coming and going took a fair amount of time since we locked up *every time* we left the house. Hopefully, the crime waves of the previous year were isolated events. We felt optimistic, feeling secure now especially with our alarms. Bill remarked their only and greatest use came about when they would blaringly remind us that we had forgotten to disarm one or more of them. I took it more seriously.

*   *   *

The Wind Chimes Hotel had been built next door to the Windsurf Resort in the early nineties by an affable contractor from Alabama. We had enjoyed watching the construction progress from our No. 312 balcony. When completed, he leased it to a German entrepreneur who managed it as an all-inclusive hotel operation, primarily servicing tourists from Germany. The hotel got into financial difficulties in the early 2000s, shortly after a chartered plane carrying all German tourists crashed in the ocean a few miles off the coast of Cabarete. It was especially devastating to Bill and me who had been partying with some of the passengers the night before their departure. I couldn't bear to walk the beach for days after hearing that suitcases and other personal items were washing onto shore. No bodies were ever recovered.

The Wind Chimes Hotel operation failed and the manager flew the coop. He was gone and the hotel was completely quiet. The Alabama contractor/owner took back the management and engaged Hugh to renovate all the apartments with the idea that the resort could then be sold. I believe Gordon and his father were hoping to be the buyers. Hugh proceeded with the extensive project.

It turned out that no one realized just how deeply in debt the manager had been or that his creditors were boiling mad. Late one afternoon, several *policía* arrived at Gordon's office packing guns and handcuffs, assuming he was connected with the fraud. Bill and I happened to be walking by the Windsurf, when we saw Gordon squeeze out of the bathroom window, and then take off at a good clip across the back lot. He later told us that even though he had explained that the debts were not his or Hugh's, he thought it better to get the hell out of there, so that was when he had politely excused himself to use the *baño*. He did not want to be arrested or involved in any way with the former manager's problems.

Alas, no one knew that the German's biggest creditor was the company who had supplied the generator which provided electricity to the entire hotel complex. The next day, when we once again began our morning stroll downtown, we saw a huge opening in the front concrete block wall of the generator enclosure, as well as the absence of the roof—and the generator. Later in the day, the scuttlebutt was that a backhoe had come sometime during the night, ripped open the housing, loaded the huge generator on a truck, and carted it away.

A couple of years later, the original owner had sorted out the debt problems, took over the hotel, divided it into condominiums, and then, one Saturday morning, put them all up for sale at very competitive prices through three realtors. The units were sold out within hours, and by Sunday night were completely under contract.

Did Hugh ever get paid for his renovation job? *Quien sabé—* who knows?

*   *   *

There was a small bakery on the main strip where they hand-squeezed oranges while you waited—one order at a time—citrus perfume filled the air. We loved to go there for an early breakfast. It was the time of day when everything came alive. From a sidewalk table, I watched street vendors arrange invitingly what they had taken from nature a few hours earlier: melons, potatoes, avocados, waxy red peppers, onions, pineapples, bananas . . . and shopkeepers hosing down the front of their stores or sweeping with brooms made of grass. We ordered *café con leche* and croissants, just out of the oven. The smell of fresh baked goods drew us like a magnet. The resident cat, seemingly unaware, wound around my leg and then stretched out on the sun-warmed tiles.

On the way back to Los Alisios, we went by way of the beach where the morning's first tourists were claiming lounge chairs for a day of sunning in front of their hotel, toting kids with sand pails and beach balls, totally slathered in lotion redolent of coconut. The ancient Haitian woman, who walked the beach *all day long* balancing a tub of freshly picked fruit on her head, was already cutting open a pineapple for a family who had called her over from their spot on the beach.

Vendors, eagerly anticipating the day's business, were setting up their shops with hand decorated clay pots, hand carved, brightly painted parrots and paintings by local or Haitian artists, usually oil on canvas with colorful, stylized scenes of Dominican life. Others were loading their display cases with necklaces and bracelets of Larimar and amber jewelry with which they would tour the beach from end to end, leaving no potential customer un-vendored.

Speaking of parrots, commonly called *Cotorro*, they are one of the most beloved birds to Dominicans. Someone told me that they saw a man beating the branches of a hibiscus bush with a stick. Abruptly the air filled with a scarlet haze, like a cyclone of vermillion confetti when a swarm of parrots were startled from its branches. How I wish I had seen that myself.

We ambled homeward, assailed by the tempting aromas coming from restaurants as they began preparing dishes for the day— especially from La Casita.

And of course, windsurfers, eyeing flapping pennants to gage the direction and force of the wind, were already gearing up. At that early hour, just beginners like us.

Should we sail today, or simply ride the surf or lounge about? Such were the weighty decisions that needed to be made in Cabarete after breakfast.

* * *

Hugh owned a rental resort designed like a motel called Las Cannas located about twelve miles east of Los Alisios. It served as his home for a number of years, as well. He told us that recently, he had been trying to lease the entire resort and that he was considering a long-term lease to a nudist club who planned to use it year round, although mostly in the winter because they were from New Hampshire. The deal didn't happen and we never really knew if Hugh had just been teasing us.

It was common knowledge that Hugh's second wife vacationed every year from Canada at his place in Las Cannas. Bill and I had met her on many occasions. Even though she had refused to grant him a divorce, he had moved ahead with his life, and had fathered, and recognized, two children by two Dominican women. He often brought the children to the Windsurf Resort where they frolicked in the pool with guests' children, ate in the restaurant, and danced by the pool. They were adorable and Hugh loved them.

* * *

Looking haggard and serious, Hugh stopped by Los Alisios one morning. I started to set up the coffee pot when he waved me away and slumped into the nearest chair. He told us that on his way home from the Windsurf Resort late the previous night he had hit a motorcycle that was travelling ahead of him on the highway . . . "*without any lights on the bike . . . totally dark; not even light colored clothing* . . . two brothers and their cousin were on board."

Hugh's hands were trembling as he spoke.

"One brother died at the scene and the other two were taken to the hospital in Puerto Plata." I put my arm around his shoulder.

"What the hell were they doing on the road without any lights? How in God's name was I supposed to see them? It was pitch black." Hugh kept shaking his head.

What could we say to console him? It was the kind of tragedy that happened all too often in the DR. It gave us an ominous feeling.

*   *   *

On our way back to the hotel from the beach one day, a young Dominican man approached us. He had a satchel full of newspapers slung over his shoulder, hawking them to sunbathers. He took one look at Bill, dropped the bag, and gave him a big bear hug. "Señor Bill, remember me? *Lionel, pintar su casa?*" He continued rapidly in his now reasonable English, to tell us that now he had *dos niños,* and in addition to his painting jobs, he sold papers to support his growing family. He still lived in the same house across from Casa Cabarete, and of course, we should come and visit to see his *familia*. We soon became regular customers whenever he spotted us on the beach, even though we had noticed that the newspapers were generally three or four days old.

One morning Bill was having lunch at Ono's with two Canadian tourists he had just met, when Lionel came up to the table from the beach, and offered the Toronto News. One of the fellows said, "Sure," and took the paper. Then he asked how much, and Lionel said forty pesos. He handed him a fifty-peso note, telling him to keep the change. Lionel just nodded at Bill, and scooted on up the beach. The Canadian, having arrived only a few days ago was eager to see what was happening at home. He suddenly looked closely at the date of the paper.

"Last Friday? Hey, I was still home then—this is old news," he exclaimed. Then with a bit of a quizzical look, "How much is fifty pesos, anyway?"

Bill shrugged, not wanting to tell him that it was about four dollars.

The man glanced down the beach for Lionel, who was long gone.

When we left the DR that year, there was Lionel at the airport terminal . . . picking up discarded papers off chairs and benches, complete or incomplete, in any language, from any country. Well, you really have to give him credit for being an industrious entrepreneur. Supply and Demand—Dominican style.

*   *   *

The following summer, one glorious afternoon at our Lakehouse in New Hampshire, the phone rang. To our surprise, it was Sandra's roommate, calling from Puerto Plata. With a shaky voice she told us that Sandra had been hit by a taxi as she was pulling out of her driveway on her motor scooter. She had been rushed to the hospital in critical condition. Witnesses said that she had flown through the air, over the taxi, and landed headfirst. Her helmet saved her life, thank God. The hospital expenses were piling up fast, and she knew that Sandra would need a lot more money than she had. Could we help?

Of course, we immediately drove into Wolfeboro where Bill wired the funds for her hospital bill. Once released, Sandra went through months of rehabilitation with terrible pain. We called often and were relieved to hear that finally she felt well enough to return to work. Sandra promised us that she now commuted strictly with friends or by taxi. The scooter was never replaced.

As my father used to say, "One little minute, and everything can change."

View of the Yard and Beach

Shary Reopens Bill's

Lynn, Nate, and Quilt

DOCE

2005 - FRIENDS AND FOES

Years had passed and Ana had prospered with her family in Casa Cabarete, living well with diligence as a good parent, guiding her children through the growing up years. It became apparent to us that she had drilled into them the importance of education when, in 2003, Danny approached Bill about the possibility of helping him and his brother Jimmy go to college.

What an unexpected surprise. We knew that they were working at a local store in the center of Cabarete, but knew nothing about their college aspirations. It would not be easy for them, as both boys needed to help support the extended family. Viannely assisted her mother with the store and although she was not interested in college, she was intent on finishing high school.

After some discussion, we decided that Bill's Books, that thriving enterprise in Cabarete, might grant a scholarship. As soon as the boys gathered the information about costs and courses to be taken, the official *Bill's Books Scholarship* program was launched.

What we offered was simple. As long as both boys got passing grades, we—oops, I mean, Bill's Books—would pay for tuition and books, but not much else. It cost about $150 US per boy per semester. The trip to the college in Puerto Plata took 45 minutes on their motorbikes. Although it was a long day because they both continued to work, they persevered, and we were really pleased when Danny graduated in 2010 with a degree in Computer Science. Jimmy went on after to law school and now has converted Ana's store into his successful law office. Bill and I are so proud of them, and their accomplishments. Ana, our Casa Cabarete friend and "tenant" had proved that a little bit of help and faith can do wonders. We are in awe of her for leading her family through the path of an underprivileged life.

*   *   *

One day, I saw Bill and Aguto out on the beach in front of Los Alisios with machetes in hand, making marks on the sand. It went on for fifteen to twenty minutes, until they came back into the yard and Aguto motored off down the street. "What's going on?" I asked.

"It's a surprise," was all Bill would say, even though he knew that I didn't like being surprised. "Tomorrow is *Domingo*. You'll find out then."

About seven-thirty Sunday morning I heard the street gate open and watched a beat-up truck loaded with palm trees back into the yard. Up pulled a car and six young boys piled out. With shovels in hand, they headed down the side passageway of the house.

So this is what he's up to, I thought, as I quickly dressed.

We had decided some time ago that all garden aspects of Los Alisios were strictly Bill's purview, and I must admit, what he had created couldn't have been more pleasurable to see.

When I got to the kitchen window, there were the first two kids, digging holes in the sand. Bill was signaling the next two, who were carrying a six-foot tall palm tree, to follow him onto the beach.

Recently, I had mentioned that it sure would be great to have palm trees in front of Los Alisios—providing shade for grandchildren and for people like me who no longer bask in the sun. But Hugh had told us that it was illegal to plant trees on the beach. "However," he had added with a wink, "the police don't work on Sunday mornings."

The truck left the yard after the trees had been unloaded, soon to return with another six trees, subject to the same routine. In all, twenty-four palms had suddenly "grown" on the beach in front of our wall, and by noon, the smiling exhausted youngsters were enjoying cokes and cookies in the shade of the *cabaña*. Aguto was proudly smiling at the job they had done, and counted out pesos for each of his helpers, as well as pocketing a neat profit for himself.

"What about this afternoon, or tomorrow," I asked, "when the *policía* come by and see what we've done? Won't Aguto, or maybe we, get into trouble?"

Smiling conspiratorially, Bill said, "That's the beauty of it. It's also illegal to *remove* any trees from the beach. So who's to say they weren't there all along? Aguto is a genius."

It was definitely time for a *siesta*.

Here's why the 'tree rules' exist in the DR. There were no laws about trees years ago, and that was okay as land was cleared for fields of sugarcane, or tobacco; perhaps converted to coconut groves. When the clearing continued for cooking or heating firewood, the Government stepped in. Wisely, they had observed the terrible deforestation in Haiti, where whole mountainsides had been clear-cut. Rather than just make a law to prevent devastation, which they did, the government subsidized *propana*, such that it was affordable for everyone. Propane filling stations were everywhere. I'd seen tanks on the back of a *moto conchos*, or being carried along the road. It was the fuel of choice. About once a month, Bill had to disconnect the large tank in our pump house and take it by taxi two miles east for a refill.

Like most rules, there are usually unintended consequences. The roots of a large tree in our front yard were clogging the septic system and its branches were completely over-shading the fruit trees we had planted. It had to go. At least that was the considered opinion of Bill and Aguto. On another early Sunday morning, there was my Paul Bunyan assisting his cohort, Aguto, lobbing off one branch at a time from the rogue tree. I guess they figured that no one would notice how it had gradually shrunk, until it was gone. That particular project required three Sunday mornings.

We chose the rationale that twenty-four new palms that had been added to the beach by far outweighed the retirement of one old duffer. It all seemed logical to me.

Another argument in favor of having planted those palms on the beach was, once they took hold, the annual erosion of sand by the higher winter tides would be greatly reduced, so we felt pretty good about that. And now, where the old tree had been, fragrant lemon and orange trees were flourishing, and bananas were hiding behind the thick scrim of bulky drooping leaves. What fun to step out the door and pick from a tree in our yard, a banana, or grapefruit for breakfast. Oh, that fresh, sweet aroma!

The prize of all plantings was a gorgeous Night Blooming Jasmine bush that Bill planted on my birthday just outside our bedroom window . . . incredibly thoughtful, my husband. When the buds opened, the air was steeped in the fragrance of crowning blossoms. It enveloped the entire yard and the intoxicating scent drifted through the window and across our bed. The perfume I use now is a blend of Lily-of-the-Valley and Jasmine which, no matter where I am, will forever take me back to Los Alisios and Cabarete.

* * *

There was absolutely no reason to own our own car in Cabarete. There were *guaguas*. There were street taxis which were one step up from *guaguas* in that they were car-size taxis that picked up no more than five passengers along the highway and charged twenty pesos rather than ten. Then there were the real taxis, like José's, which with one call was at your service. And of course, in town, you could always walk.

So why did Bill feel he needed a car?

He wouldn't say exactly, but he did want one, and the next thing I knew, he had located a beat up 1992 Mazda and bought it. I felt badly for José to lose our business . . . he had become a friend and had driven us wherever we wanted to go.

The first thing we learned was that parking a car adjacent to the ocean in the beating sun is not very good for the car, and so a canvas cover was the first accessory purchased. Then there was the deflated tire, which required a trip to Sosúa in a *guagua* to purchase a foot pump. And while Bill was there . . . a tire gauge, a lug wrench, a set of socket wrenches, and a reflective windshield screen . . . small cost items, to be sure, but increasing the car investment dollars by about twenty percent.

What had been the packed dirt front yard of Los Alisios needed to be covered with white gravel to act as the protected parking area inside our gated property. Since the house was only eighteen feet back from the gate, it required considerable maneuvering to get the car in or out of the yard. Bill was undaunted.

We did take a few trips around town: Sosúa for lunch, a few Atlantic Book Club meetings, and even drove to Tropicoco for their international buffet, which heretofore had been a healthy walk from Los Alisios.

But then, what to do with the car when it was time to head home?

Resourceful Bill found a friendly German mechanic who had lived in the States and had actually done some work on the car. He said he'd be glad to keep it at his place, run it occasionally to keep the battery charged, and the cost per month was minimal. When it was time to go to the airport, he gladly drove us (in our car) and gave us his email address to let him know when we would return.

The following December, "the car man" met us at the airport, drove us back to his place, and jumped out. Handing an invoice through the window, he said: "no rush." As we pulled away, I noticed a car in his yard that looked in great shape, balanced up on cement blocks.

At Los Alisios, unpacked and settled in, Bill looked over the invoice, and started to sputter: Eleven thousand pesos? Then he went out to check the Mazda. What the Hell! *Seven thousand miles more on the speedometer?* It became obvious that "the car man" had preserved his own car and used ours the entire time we were gone. When Bill returned to confront him, his explanation was that the best way to keep a car in good running shape was to run it. We couldn't argue too much with that, but when he realized that Bill was upset, he reduced the invoice by half and gave some credit against the storage cost.

That night, just as Bill was drifting off to sleep, he said: "Do you think he rented our Mazda out and made money on it to boot?"

I chose not to respond.

Within the month, Bill sold the Mazda. José gladly assisted in the sale and was most pleased that we were his customers once again.

* * *

Semana Santa or Holy Week (aka Easter) was one of the most celebrated holidays in the DR. Beginning on Wednesday or Thursday, it was a *tranquillo* time for reflection and prayer. On Friday, there were enactments in the streets when a few men depicting Judas dressed up in funny costumes and children, rattling tin cans, chased them as punishment for "selling Jesus." The excitement was whether Judas could elude his chasers. A parade led by a *Judas* would march down the street or suddenly traipse into a restaurant, dancing along between the tables, followed by up to twenty revelers. Waiters would frown, laugh, and dodge as best they could. It was a wild, colorful, and noisy event full of action and excitement. Best of all, I loved watching the children having such fun.

The day before Semana Santa began, all official offices and banks were closed down. We had learned years ago that if we needed cash from an ATM and hadn't taken it by Wednesday, we'd be out of luck, and money, until the following Tuesday since every available peso in the machines had already been withdrawn. Also, our *cambia* on the street was either cleaned out or charging whatever exchange rate he could get away with. Being a favored, regular customer only went so far for us during Semana Santa.

Saturday and Sunday was when the *real* celebration began. Hotels were filled to capacity by wealthy Dominicans from Santo Domingo, and Cabarete positively heaved with parties and people who were extremely *borracho*. The government sent Marshals into town that lined the roads and walked the beaches, because in a country that had few seriously enforced driving laws, Dominicans *did* drink and drive. The Marshals would stand with red flags attempting to slow down traffic. But by Sunday, after one or two of them had been brushed by passing cars or busses, they had been known to give up the fight, and join in the festivities.

Bill and I didn't learn the full impact of the holiday until the year we moved into Los Alisios. It was then that we became intimately involved with the extent of celebration and how it affected us as homeowners bordering the beach. It would begin when five or six busses parked on the street blocking our driveway and entrance gate. Then hundreds of happy Dominicans debarked with coolers, grills, blankets, and many excited children. They flocked to the beach and took it over . . . the entire beach. Like Coney Island. We braced ourselves each year for the busiest, craziest week in Cabarete.

Fortunately, windsurfing was restricted, *by the government,* to narrow, cordoned-off sections of the beach during that entire week to prevent collisions with swimmers, by accident or due to drunkenness.

I'm not sure what the word for litter is in Spanish, but that is the only description I could use for the completely *littered* beach at the end of each day. Trash of every kind would be scattered over every square foot. The restaurants and hotels had crews to rake up the mess directly in front of them, but *not* in front of Los

Alisios. Instead, thinking we were smart, we put out huge trash barrels, but the hint went largely unnoticed even though whole families would settle in and make themselves comfortable under the palms that we had planted. Usually, when the holiday was over and done, Bill and Aguto's crew had to do a thorough cleaning. Pretty much filling his truck for a dump run.

On the positive side, children romped in the ocean, their lean, bronzed bodies playful with laughter and teasing. Each family set up picnic areas with delicious smells of *pollo quisada* (fried chicken, garlic, and red onions), wafting on the sea breeze. They relaxed on lounges, enjoying the day together as hot rhythms of Merengue and Bachata music beat across the sand.

I loved watching the graceful, lithe teenage boys, kicking, jumping, and wrestling each other to the ground as they rolled in sand, their smiles dazzled with laughter. Rough and tumble but all so gentle—light, cocoa-colored arms and legs flailing, glistening in the ocean—*compadres*.

That aspect was heartwarming to see, but on the other hand we were held hostage in our house and I felt selfish with our crystal clear swimming pool and gardens in full bloom all fenced and gated. The first year we lived in Los Alisios, a few strangers came off the beach asking to use our *baño,* and we said yes. BIG MISTAKE. The stream of users went through eight rolls of toilet paper and we had to have the septic tank pumped out after the weekend. Fortunately, we had directed them to the *baño* in the pump house; that yard-accessible *baño* had been suggested by Aguto, for himself and other workers.

When hearing about our misplaced hospitality, Gordon and Hugh and Carol and Socorro, plus all our other friends, warned us that "opening our home" could be an invitation to case our property. A warning we later learned should have been heeded more closely.

*   *   *

Brother Dort and his wife Medi came to visit four or five times over the years: once they stayed in No. 312 and thereafter, in the lockout apartment at Los Alisios, so they were right in tune with our adventure, if not every step we took along the way.

The last time they came, exhausted from the day of travel, we had all retired early for the night, when suddenly, Medi began knocking urgently on our bedroom door. "Sorry to wake you, but you've GOT TO come see something truly spectacular."

We bounded out of bed and followed her as she rushed on ahead of us. Standing between the swimming pool and the flower gardens, she pointed toward the sky out over the ocean.

With great reverence, she said, "**Moon over Cabarete!** Isn't it romantic? It just couldn't be any fuller. I feel as though I could reach out and touch it. "

Bill and I looked up. Oh yes, there it was . . . a bright, perfectly round yellow globe of light against the midnight sky, except . . . it happened to be the newly installed lamp atop a slender black pole at the far corner of our property. Cabarete officials had just the week before installed it to provide light and safety on that section of the beach for late night strollers.

To this day, we still laugh about it, and haven't let Medi forget her magnificent moon over Cabarete.

*   *   *

Ian and Lynn were among our Canadian friends who had wonderful tales to tell of having worked and traveled all over the world: he as a Project Engineer, and she as a teacher. Quite a number of years prior to retirement, they had purchased a house directly on Cabarete beach, about eight hundred feet east of Los Alisios. They ran it as a year-round guesthouse, catering to single, avid windsurfers. Gabby managed it in their absence. Escaping the winter months in Canada, they lived on the first floor of their Cabarete house, renting out the second floor bedrooms. Occasionally, if there was a strong demand, they would even rent the first floor and catch an off-the-beach hotel room for themselves. There was a grill and a small hut in the side yard. Tables and chairs were set up where they held cookouts for the adventurers from Europe and Canada who rented year after year to pursue their passion . . . windsurfing.

Soon after arriving one year, Ian announced that he had gone to bartending school over the summer and was now working on modifications to the hut in his yard, transforming it to a native-looking bar, to be called *Wilson's Beach Bar*. His idea was to make a little money, plus have fun by attracting locals and vacationers who would arrive by the beach, looking for exotic—or not so exotic—drinks from 5 to 7 pm only. After all, he didn't want to work too hard.

"I love to hear everyone's stories," Ian told us. "It will be a lot of fun."

The Grand Opening was by invitation only. On the appointed day, we dressed up for the occasion and strolled the short distance down the beach for the launching of the soon-to-be-famous Wilson's Beach Bar. Lynn had told us that this entire idea was strictly Ian's deal; she emphasized *strictly,* and that she was *not* going to have any part in it.

Just as we climbed the few steps up from the beach and opened the small gate leading to their lawn, we could hear Ian shout: "Lynn. I need more ice." He was standing behind the bar, calling out over the heads of his customers. "Hurry—and I need a bottle opener, too." There was quite a crowd.

As we waited to be served, Ian yelled again, this time with a bit more panic in his voice: "More glasses, Lynn. We need lots more."

Waiting patiently, I noticed that in this rush of business, Ian wasn't following one of the cardinal rules learned in Basic Bartending: *always measure the liquor carefully*. Instead, he was splashing great amounts of booze over ice, then, with a debonair flourish of a swizzle, handing the concoction across the bar. He certainly would have return customers if for no other reason than for serving drinks with such a wallop, although I don't think that was his intention. As more commands were issued, Lynn rushed in and out of the house. Bill and I could only grin at each other knowingly.

We were chatting with a fascinating couple from Kenya beneath the massive tree that shaded most of the yard when suddenly something plopped directly into my drink with a splash that soaked the front of my blouse. Whatever it was, it apparently had fallen from the branches above. It startled me to the point of emitting a loud yelp before I scrutinized my glass. There, I saw the cutest little gecko face looking up at me. It was incredible that he had fallen from fifteen feet above, right into my glass with a diameter of no more than two and one-half inches. Just like a hole-in-one.

Someone in the startled crowd said, "What's a gecko doing in your drink?"

Our Kenyan friend observed the little fellow, and instantly quipped: "Why, swimming, of course." Everyone shrieked with laughter; then Ian called out from behind the bar: "That's it, folks, we've just been re-christened . . . ***Wilson's Gecko Bar.***"

Alert, the gecko watches with
tiny black eyes, pebbles in a river.
He makes a dipping motion of his head,
dainty and quick, a leaf moved by a puff of wind.
I long to stroke my fingers across his smooth
underside, to feel the secret beat
of his tiny heart, the pulse of life,
the vibration in all living things.
As I lean forward, he flicks his body around,
a flash of green, and he darts out of sight.
Gone into a crevice of shadow,
gone to the earth.

Speaking of geckos, there were several who frequented our *cabaña*, especially when I was stretched out on a lounge, reading and snacking. I discovered that they like pieces of crackers, which I crumbled and tossed down next to me. Cautiously, they'd take a piece in their mouth and hurry to the shade of a flower. I loved watching them.

*   *   *

Not long before we had left for the DR that year (2005) Bill had said he was tired of hearing me complain about my hair . . . how it always frizzed in hot weather. "What about a wig?" he said. "It just might solve your problem."

That very afternoon I chose a honey-colored Farrah Fawcett wig at a shop in Portsmouth. I cannot explain how glamorous and *young* it made me feel. And look. As soon as I returned home, I put it on and knocked on a neighbor's door across the street.

When he opened the door, he hesitated a moment, then said, as if to a Mary Kay salesperson: "May I help you?" I loved that he didn't recognize me.

Once we settled in Cabarete, I had several similar reactions, but perhaps the best one was when cousin Wally and Dee Dee from Long Island were staying with us at Los Alisios. The four of us had spent the day together visiting, eating, and playing games under the *cabaña* and then it was siesta time. The plan for the evening was to get gussied up and have dinner across the street.

By scheme, I was to hide in Bill's Books in the foyer waiting for Wally to come out of the lockout. When he did, Bill would tell him that I had gone ahead to make a reservation.

That was my cue: I boldly sashayed into the living room, wig, and all. Bill introduced me to Wally as "our good friend, Wendy," whom we had invited to join us for dinner. Here's how the conversation went from there:

Wally: *I'm so happy to meet you, Wendy.* Shook hands.

Wendy: *I'm delighted to be joining you for the evening.*

Wally: *Are you visiting, or do you live here?*

Wendy: *No . . . I live here.*

Wally: *Oh, and ah, what do you do here?*

Wendy: *I'm a streetwalker.* (Please don't ask me where that came from)

Wally: Silence for moment, and then: *And which side of the street do you walk on?*

Wendy: *Well. I don't think that's very funny.*

Wally: *I, I didn't mean it that way. Oh. Here comes my girlfriend. Dee Dee, please come over here dear, and meet Julie and Bill's friend, Wendy. She's joining us for dinner.*

I had all I could do to keep from screaming with laughter. I couldn't look at Bill. On the way across the street, he leaned over and whispered: "We've got to tell them."

Just at that moment, Wally draped his arm over my shoulder, and then reached down and gave my fanny a sassy pinch. Boy, at age 82—and a distant cousin—he sure still had a lot of moxie.

Our explanation burst forth when we were all seated at the table, while Felix, bless his heart, patiently waited to take our order for dinner.

A great wig. No frizz—and lots of laughs to boot.

*   *   *

Elizabeth now worked at a large all-inclusive hotel chain at the eastern end of the beach. She often walked the nearly half mile up to Los Alisios after work to join us for dinner or just for a coke and a snack before hailing a *guagua* to return home to her three children, about seven miles further east. We always enjoyed this time together. She is so affectionate, never asking for anything (which of course makes me want to give her everything.) Although neither one had made the big effort to learn the other's language, we got along great with a well-used dictionary sitting on the table between us.

One day Bill and I invited her and the kids, plus her brother Luis who lived next door to her with their mother, to come over on Sunday for lunch and a swim in the pool. She nodded and we agreed on 12:30, right after she came home from church.

Bill and I were ready by 12:15, and then we waited. And waited. Finally they arrived around 2:00 pm. Two loaded *guaguas* pulled up in front of the house. We watched with mouths agape, as Elizabeth, her mother, her sister, her brother, and sixteen children disembarked. It took me a while of chatting with her, but I finally understood her explanation: word had gotten out as to where they were going, and all the neighborhood children stood around Elizabeth's house, crying. "Can we go, too? *Por favor?*"

What could she do? What could we do?

Bill ran down to Janet's to buy a lot more food and drinks for the picnic, while the kids had a blast frolicking in the pool, and I very nervously acted as lifeguard. Elizabeth and her mother went straight to the kitchen to prepare a ton of sandwiches and a big platter of fruit . . . all to be served with cokes and lemonade. Even so, it was hard to lure the children from the pool. I had made brownies and Bill had picked up a couple of quarts of ice cream.

After the happy, tired little people filed back onto a *guaguas* four hours later, with their enthusiastic *muchas gracias*, we retreated into the house, surveyed all our wet towels in a heap and a kitchen that looked like a storm had passed through, and then turned toward the bedroom door with a mutual nod. *Mas tardes,* that elastic Dominican time measurement. Or maybe even *mañana.*

* * *

We always hated to leave our idyllic winter home, but the magnetic pull of spring in New Hampshire had its way with us by mid-April. By then, early perennial gardens and wild lilies-of-the-valley were on our minds. Spring, my most favorite season of all.

Knowing that José would be whisking us off to the airport at nine thirty in the morning, our suitcases were packed and sitting near the front door, although the lids were up to receive last minute items. Most of the day had been spent in closing-up activities: cleaning the refrigerator, going over gardening needs and wishes with Aguto, etc. At Los Alisios, our *"watchy-man"* was Socorro, who, unlike Roque, was a trusted and efficient manager in our absence. She took care of everything for us.

The last thing we did was to push all the furniture in the living room into the center of the room and drape it with sheets. As the queen of organization, I finally announced to Bill that essentially, everything was done, and we should go out for one last dinner on the beach.

Wanting to say goodbye to René, we planned to cap off the day at Ocean Taste. Even though we'd be just a three-minute walk from Los Alisios, we locked all the doors and gates behind us. Fort Knox had nothing on us.

I always enjoyed sitting on the restaurant's patio, soothed by the ocean's waves and the chatter of diners in the background. After a succulent meal of fresh *mahi-mahi* broiled on a grill set under the stars, we bid farewell to René, Roberto, and the servers we had come to know and like over the winter.

We returned to Los Alisios about ten pm. Bill opened the large sliding gate at the street, then padlocked it behind us. Because of the recent break-ins around Cabarete, we had gotten into the habit of fully locking up every time we left the house. He next opened the bookstore gate, then padlocked it behind us. While he was doing that, I opened the house door with my key, walked in a few feet, and suddenly locked eyes with an intruder who was standing about twenty-five feet away, next to the kitchen bar. I yelled out in a voice unfamiliar to me: "Bill, there's a man in here!"

Boy, did that start Bill's engine. He dashed past me. The robber dropped whatever he was about to steal and started toward the sliding glass doors leading to the back gardens. Bill tore around the pile of furniture in the middle of the room, reached under a sheet, and grabbed a dining room chair. Holding it out in front of him like a lion trainer, he charged at the robber.

"He's got a knife," I yelled like the announcer at a sporting event, hoping that Bill would back off. But, oh, no. Bill made another lunge, jabbing the robber in the chest and then, stepping to the side, he lost his footing and landed on his back.

But only for a second.

Fortunately, instead of attacking once again when Bill was down, the robber used that time trying to unlock the slider.

Bill bounced back on his feet and recovered the chair. He emitted a roar, the sound of which I had never heard from a human being, and charged again. All I could think of was how carefully we had *locked ourselves in*.

When the robber poked his knife through the rungs of the chair and I saw blood on Bill's arm, I started toward the kitchen for a bigger, longer knife than his. But then, when the robber turned threateningly toward me, blocking my path, I stopped in my tracks.

"Let him go!" I screamed at Bill, as I stepped back.

More sparring, more blood. It seemed that Bill was trying to get to the sliding door too, and then I realized that he kept his gardening machete to the left of the door, out of sight. I didn't want to think what would happen if he got his hands on it.

"Please, let him get out." I yelled again to Bill, when I saw that the attack with the chair was hitting its mark. The robber, a young kid, obviously had not expected a madman as an adversary. He looked terrified.

A knife versus a chair. One knife thrust caught Bill in his chest, fairly near his heart. Blood appeared on his shirt. Now I was ready to join the fight. Bill took a millisecond to look down at his chest; that hesitation allowed the robber just time enough to release the door latch and unlocked the slider. He pushed it open and shot out the door.

Bill dropped the chair, grabbed the machete from its hiding spot, and sprinted across the yard after him, brandishing it over his head. The robber raced toward the ocean through the *cabaña* and, in a motion that might have won an Olympic medal, grasped the upper rail of the *spiked fence*, and vaulted over it and onto the beach. Bill stopped at the gate, thank God.

The aftermath was quite uneventful. We saw where the intruder had smashed the kitchen window and climbed through the small opening above the sink. Shattered glass was all over the counter and floor. It was also clear now why he had not tried to go out the way he had come in. I figured he was a novice since the first thing a seasoned robber would do, in my opinion, would be to determine a speedy departure. Like . . . unlock the slider *before* he started rummaging around.

Raising Bill's shirt, I saw that his numerous puncture wounds on his chest and arms were, *gracias a Dios*, quite superficial. So we hurried back to Ocean Taste. While we explained what had happened, my hands were shaking as if palsied. René called the *policía* and then followed us back to the house. I put dressings on Bill's wounds while we waited. The armed *policía* finally showed up in their starched shirts, khakis, and combat boot, looked all around, pointed to the broken window, and said, "*Si*".

They decided it definitely wasn't an inside job, and asked if anyone disliked us? Wished us harm? We said no. They took our descriptions of the young man, for whatever they were worth, and we never heard another word about the event.

Some expat friend had said to us, when we built Los Alisios, that the distance between those Americans who were comfortable living in the DR and those who were not, was a precipice upon which we stood . . . "the ground beneath, subject to erosion at any moment." At the time, we didn't believe them.

Once we were alone, and the broken glass was swept up, Bill guzzled down a half bottle of rum and slept like a baby. I, on the other hand, sat bolt upright in bed the entire night, aware of every little squeak and sigh of the palm trees. Moonlight fell into the room like bits of mica.

José came at nine in the morning. Before he arrived, Bill had called Hernando-the-metal-man and arranged for installation of two more gates, iron bars on all the windows, and all new locks. The whole episode truly demoralized us. Our haven had been violated. Our personal beings had been violated. I was sad and frightened. We had a lot of thinking to do about our future in Cabarete.

At home, I dreamed about the fight. It was horrifying . . . to even contemplate what could have happened.

Elizabeth's Pool Party

Bill's Books Scholarship Recipient – Danny with Thania

Wilson's Gecko Bar

TRECE

2006 - THE BLUSH IS OFF THE ROSE

The summer and fall of 2005 in New Hampshire passed quickly, but not without the recurring vision of the frightening knife fight last April. The converse of that is when you recount a tale often enough, it can become less than it was—relegated to an almost amusing experience. Even so, just below the surface, the picture of blood seeping through Bill's shirt was indelibly carved across my memory's screen.

Thus, armed with three extra-large cans of long distance hornet spray, and a never-been-used pepper spray dispenser from when my girls were in high school, Bill and I returned to Cabarete in December determined to resume the lifestyle we had grown accustomed to at Los Alisios. Interestingly enough, we noticed the absence of clapping upon our arrival, which, in a strange way, added to my anxiety.

After José dropped us off at Los Alisios, I felt a shiver of misgiving until we saw all the additional security measures that "Hernando- the-iron-man" had installed over the windows and doors in our absence. After placing new batteries in the motion detectors, we began to unwind and settle in.

*   *   *

Our first day on the beach, we observed that kite boarding had definitely taken hold. As with windsurfing, it also harnessed the power of the wind to propel you across the water, but in a whole new way.

I knew that some time ago Gordon had purchased beachfront land out on a point at the far eastern end of Cabarete beach and named it Ocean Point. Together with Hugh, he and his father had built a luxury condo complex with panoramic views of the ocean, which became, over the past year, peppered with rainbows of kite sails. The area in front of his condos was referred to as Kite Beach.

"It wasn't easy to learn how to kite board," Gordon enthused, "but what a thrill, once you get the hang of it. It's going worldwide, and will probably surpass windsurfing. That's why we located on the point. The beach to the west of us is aligned perfectly for kiting, and the old beach to the east is just the opposite. Cabarete will be the best of both worlds. I love it."

Multiple kite boarding "schools" were evidenced all along the beach. First they had to pump air into the sail sections of the kite, and then stretch 100 feet of flying lines along the beach. It was hell trying to take our late afternoon walk through such an obstacle course. We definitely passed those open classrooms at our own peril. The instructors, usually with the aid of a young Dominican lad, had the students practice running along the beach trying to become airborne and then to land it, or be dragged into the shallow surf. It seemed like a really dangerous sport so I was glad to see that all students were decked out with helmets and flotation vests, and I was relieved that Bill decided to stay with windsurfing. Stevie, my adventuresome son, even though he had returned from his lessons with bruises and scrapes on his shins, had said it was fabulous fun. The beach was alive with the new sport, bringing more students, observers, and vendors to Cabarete. Business was thriving.

It's nearly impossible to describe the new downtown Cabarete—the wonderful chaos of it. A riot of colors amidst open shops, drooping telephone wires, cars double-parked, pulsing music, drivers clustered by their taxis, cell phones at every ear, tantalizing smells from cafés and restaurants, people and dogs passing on narrow uneven sidewalks, laughter, smiles, congeniality. A marvelous potpourri of humanity.

By the time we returned to Los Alisios, after a dinner of artichoke and mushroom pizzas at French Alley, we felt relaxed and relieved that all seemed secure. We slept like logs to sounds of the surf's soft murmur.

* * *

The next morning at Ocean Taste for breakfast, we went over our calendar, reviewing and scheduling visitors coming to visit this season. In addition to our monthly Book Club dates, the calendar filled rapidly. Without elaboration, or necessarily in the right sequence, let me list them here: Danny and Tina from California,

Barbara and Scott from Arizona, Pixie and Donna from Maine, as well as grandson Michael and buddies. Our New Hampshire neighbors Roberta and Richard, Heather and Len, and Greg, our Lakehouse neighbor. That rounded out the first time visitors, for whom a lot of thought and planning of activities were going to be a must.

Then there were the repeats . . . Ann and John, Lynn, Nate, Emily, Sarah, Shary and Bobby, Julie and Ari, Elan, Talia, Medi and Dort, Liz, Nancy and Doug, Wally and Dee Dee, Stevie, Lena and Roshana, and their friends Dan, Christina, Jonathan, and Juliet, and grandsons, Brian and Douglas, hopefully with Kyle this time. They would be easy, as they were familiar with the country and our living style; but some planning was required nonetheless. In addition to our houseguests, we were looking forward to seeing our dear friends Eileen and Paul who were coming in March. This was to be indeed, a very busy season, and we were eager for it!

At this, our first breakfast of the season, and on my final cup of potent Dominican coffee, I reminded Bill that I definitely intended to finish my novel, *Silent Cry*, before returning to New Hampshire, to which he retorted that he had four or five *Opinions* yet to write for *Rye Reflections*. I'm not absolutely sure, but I seem to recollect that we stood up, paid the bill, and with daunting calendar in hand, hurried ourselves back up the beach, through the sliding gate to the *cabaña* and into the lounge chairs for an early *siesta*.

*   *   *

Based on the number of up-to-date titles on the shelves in Bill's Books which had been open Monday, Wednesday, and Friday under Karen's careful eye, I could see that it had thrived in our absence. Bill soon developed the habit of setting out the *open* signs on the street and beach whenever we were going to be around for the day. My loquacious husband loved to converse with the tourists from around the world. He'd watch over a customer's shoulder as they signed his ongoing visitor's log. Noting where they were from, he'd run his finger down the list and then ask if they knew *so-and-so* who had signed two years before from the same city or state. Ignoring the "are you nuts" look from most, once in a while he scored with a "Wow! When were *they* here?"

I believe Bill got that gift of gab from his mother, Daisy. Sometimes I found myself hooked into the shopkeeper role, and must admit that once a conversation had started, it really wasn't all that bad. That's from the reticent, introverted me.

Wilson's Gecko Bar was open; however Ian had some complaints about a group of kids who had begun playing beach baseball daily, right in front of the bar, which discouraged customers due to both noise and errant balls. By the season's end, he decided that it was time to wrap up the adventure. What a shame.

*   *   *

After a week had passed, Bill asked José to go with him while he checked out his investment in a motor-scooter shop just east of town run by one William Sonck from Brussels and his wife. The previous year, Maria had convinced us to back him since she was a part-owner. An hour later, Bill returned with a long face. The conversation he had had with William in his *vacated* shop had been brief. There were no bikes, no tools, no money, only a dejected and defeated William. It seems that the remaining inventory, which in theory should have belonged to my Bill since he had advanced the money for it, had been confiscated by the manufacturer due to lack of monthly payments. The excuse by William that he and his wife had to eat was about all the explanation given in unintelligible Belgian/German/Spanish (English now completely gone). It must be a Dominican disease— the sudden loss of ability to communicate in a formerly fluent language. We didn't think there was any recourse other than Dominican legal, which would be pure torture. Bill decided to swallow the loss. Never again, we vowed . . . never again.

* * *

Progress toward the completion of The Palace next door to Los Alisios continued, but was slow, annoying, noisy, and frustrating; and Pequeño Refugio, the hotel on the other side of us, was undergoing another complete renovation. It was discouraging to be surrounded by re-bar, cement, workers, and more than a little noise. We ignored it as best we could, and concentrated each day on what had been planned on our calendar entries—one at a time.

Los Alisios was the wondrous oasis in the middle of overbearing buildings, dwarfed by the construction, and inundated with leering itinerant workers who ate and slept on the job site. We tried hard to not allow it to bother us.

In conversation on the beach one day, one of the investors in Valero asked Bill why we didn't consider developing our site into a hotel/condo as well. The thought of reverting back to our original plan seemed out of the question. Almost laughable. Besides, we were having just too much fun running our friends-only hotel without the responsibility or headaches that come with owning a multi-unit building.

However, the seed had been planted and a few days later, probably at a time when conversation in the *cabaña* was nearly impossible due to construction clamor, Bill asked me if I had any interest in selling to a developer, and what price I would consider. I was shocked at first, but did think about it. The idea germinated in the back of my mind. And I'm sure, Bill's, too.

*   *   *

One day in mid February, Bill and Paul didn't get started windsurfing until late morning. After a half-hour or so, Paul had had enough and called it a day, while Bill thought he wanted to go on a bit longer. A big mistake. The wind had become too strong, past his expertise, and no matter how hard he tried to sail back to shore, he was carried down toward the western end of the beach. He fell, drifted, climbed back on and lifted the sail, only to be knocked down again. After eight to ten falls, he just let the wind push him westward until he reached Bozo Beach. Almost all beginners ended up there, one time or another. Later, he told me that he was really bummed because he didn't consider himself a beginner any longer. Exhausted with the effort of trying *not* to land there, Bill had dragged his sailing rig in the shallow water, about three-quarters of a mile, all the way back to the BIC Center where he had rented his equipment.

Unaware of Bill's sailing fiasco, I entered the beach scene with Eileen and Paul who had showered and changed. We planned to catch lunch at the café in French Alley. When I saw Bill, he looked bedraggled, although he was game for lunch together. We gave our order to the waitress and then chatted away for almost an hour sitting on the uncushioned metal chairs. Apparently the waitress had forgotten to give our order to the kitchen. I looked at Bill who nodded that he was willing to wait longer. The sandwiches finally came. Bill was feeling sore from his struggle on the water, and when he stood to head home, he groaned and then limped along as we made our way down the beach, back to Los Alisios.

The next morning, Bill literally could not walk. Knowing that there was a small medical center downtown—Stevie had once taken Roshana there with an upset stomach—I called big strong José for a taxi ride in hopes of finding a doctor on duty. Even though it was less than a quarter mile from the house, I asked

José to please wait for us. Bill would not have been able to walk even that short distance back home.

We lucked out. Larry, an expat American-turned-Dominican chiropractor, was on duty. By one of those strange coincidences, Larry had been on the beach several weeks before, when the man to whom we had rented our No. 312 Condo at the Windsurf Resort, had broken his neck when he flipped while trying to ride a wave. Larry had witnessed the accident and took charge. He immediately stretched the surfer out on a windsurf board and facilitated a fast trip to the hospital in Puerto Plata, where a halo and traction were applied; all of which saved our Canadian renter's life. We had heard all about that scary event on the beach, but did not know that Larry had been the hero until friends of the young Canadian came to Cabarete to gather his belongings.

I'm sure Bill told Larry about his own broken neck that he had acquired when showing off with a dive from a pier in New Jersey in 1948. Seems he forgot he was doing racing dives in 30 inch deep water, and as a pretty girl strolled by, he suddenly performed a jackknife and crumpled on the sandy bottom. I often think about how lucky he was whenever I watch him now with so much love and admiration, windsurfing, or building extensions to our Lakehouse.

Larry told us that Bill had a misalignment in his hip saddle. He performed manipulation four days in a row, then three times a week for the next three weeks, and then twice a week until Bill was "cured." We were oh, so grateful. José drove Bill forth and back for the first three weeks of treatment. Fortunately, Larry considered Bill as a "local" and the charge was extremely reasonable: $500 pesos RD . . . about $15 US per visit. (Eat your heart out, Medicare).

Larry also recommended massage after each treatment, and fortunately we were able to engage Lisa, an expat massage therapist from Massachusetts. Since Bill still had trouble walking, she accommodated us by coming to Los Alisios using the "lock-out" living room for privacy. She left an extra massage table for in-between "house calls." On more than a few occasions she had some of her other clients come to our house for treatment since her office was out of town. I served iced tea and cookies to all her clients. My mother would have approved.

To this day, Bill still does the exercises Larry and Lisa recommended before getting out of bed each morning, and his hip has not gone out since that time. TG. He even has me doing them now, and my chronic sciatica that comes and goes doesn't bother me nearly as much.

Bill still windsurfs at age 82. Thank you, again, Larry.

*   *   *

The Windsurf Resort occasionally had a group of vendors set up around the pool, and when Steve and family were here, I asked Roshana if she'd like to go across the street with me to look around, maybe find a treasure to take home with her. Stevie came with us, and because I'm always in a hurry even when I'm not in a hurry, I strode ahead to lead the way. I tripped off an unexpected step and fell, putting all my weight on my tuned ankle. The left one. Again. The same one I had broken several years past, also at the Windsurf. I sat on a chair while Roshana chose a hand-painted parrot, I think, and then, between Stevie and Bill, I hopped my way across the street back to Los Alisios.

Iced, elevated, and multicolored, my ankle continued to expand and by morning I could not put any weight on it. Having been foolishly cavalier with the last break, this time we conscientiously pursued medical attention. The local doctor sent us to have an x-ray. Four miles out of town, we turned onto a dirt road ending at a cement block building with *Médico* written on the one door. There was a man who greeted us wearing a dazzlingly white coat and a serious expression. He took one look at my bloated ankle and said: "*radiografía.*"

He called something in rapid Spanish and a young boy, probably no more than 16, appeared at the door, beckoning me to follow him. He also had a white coat on. We stepped out the door, took a left, and entered an open room that held a gurney and a large, rusted, behemoth of a machine. He took two x-rays, disappeared, came back, took two more x-rays, came back, and started to pull the machine once again over my ankle when I said *alto* in a very commanding voice. He said, *no bueno, Señiora . . .* or something like that. He left and returned immediately with the doctor (I had to assume he was a doctor). And then, incredibly, the doctor took hold of the toe next to my baby toe, and pulled with all his might. Then exclaimed in recognizable English: "No broke. *Seriedad spen."* Serious sprain??

Two hundred pesos and a pair of crutches later we were on our way back to Cabarete.

Upon our return to New Hampshire, a *real* x-ray determined that my ankle had definitely been broken and had already begun to heal, slightly out of line. I had to wear a boot for three weeks.

The toe that the quack pulled still turns purple in the shower and in extreme cold.

So much for x-rays in the DR. And *Medicos.*

*　　*　　*

On a quiet Sunday morning (no construction next door) we were eating breakfast in the *cabaña.* Soon after saying *adios* to the last of our long list of this season's visitors, I said to Bill, "Why don't we gather information together about possibly selling. Just in case . . ."

He replied, shifting his aching back, "Good idea . . . just in case. Do you realize we started out that way six years ago, when we first saw that *For Sale* sign on the corrugated fence?" I nodded, and he continued: "Number one, we are surrounded by giant buildings. Number two, we are getting older and the medical care down here sucks. (Forgive me, Larry). Number three, we have been robbed, invaded, and in a knife duel, which I'm not sure that I would win should it happen again." My heart leaped into full arrhythmia at the thought. "So, I agree," he went on, "let's sit down with a realtor this afternoon. But let's not forget, we've had a most incredible twenty years in the DR . . . and we still have the 40 weeks-a-year Time Share." My Billy reached across the space between us and took my hand in his . . . the adventure seekers. We continued to discuss the idea, and did in fact, gather all the information we needed that very afternoon.

*   *   *

As the end of April arrived, Bill's back was given a clean bill of health by Larry and Lisa. My ankle only ached when it rained, or when I walked too far. We had our final Atlantic Book Club meeting for the year, hosted a dinner at Ocean Taste for all our Dominican friends and families, visited Casa Cabarete and said farewell to Ana and family, and had our parting drinks at Wilson's Gecko Bar.

We also sat with Gordon and Hugh in the Windsurf Resort office and learned of their potential plans for what Gordon called Windsurf Resort Phase III: six new buildings on the lot next door that he had purchased years ago (aided by the money we had paid for the forty years of timeshare??). It sounded exciting and we really wished him well.

Aguto and Bill went over the weekly garden routine. And finally, our trusted friends, Sandra, Socorro, and Elizabeth, came to Los Alisios for a last visit and review of the house-care instructions, hugs, and a teary *adiós*.

José arrived just as we stood in the *cabaña* for a last moment. The air was fully saturated with the scent of the ocean. I closed my eyes and inhaled. Bill stood behind me, encircling me with his strong, reassuring arms.

It had been a mixed season, yet we said to all as we pulled away: "See you in December."

Our Living Room

The Lock-Out

The Palace Closing Us In

CATORCE

2006 - THE END OF A DREAM

Out of the blue, a Canadian friend called us at the Lakehouse to tell us that Hugh was dead. "Hugh was murdered. It's all over the Winnipeg papers."

I couldn't speak. I hung up and ran to tell Bill, crying my heart out. Our friend, the man who built Los Alisios was gone. His talent and ebullience snuffed out in the night.

Once we calmed ourselves, I called her back. She said that everyone thought it had to do with the accident that happened almost two years before when Hugh had struck a *motor concho* on his way home. One boy had died. One was in a wheelchair for life, the other unscathed. A year later, the family had taken Hugh to court hoping to be awarded a lot of money, but the judgment came back against them because the bike had had no lights or reflectors. The judge surmised that it would have been impossible to have been visible at that hour. Our friend said that the papers were calling it a clear case of revenge and that the authorities had already jailed several members of that family.

"His throat had been slit as he slept in his bedroom while his wife and one of his Dominican daughters were held captive in the next room. The police apprehended three boys walking down the beach not far from Hugh's house at Las Cannas reportedly with blood on their clothes."

Bill and I could barely sleep that night. First thing in the morning, we called Gordon.

He had quite a different account of what he thought had happened to his father. He said that when he received a call from the police, he rushed in the middle of the night to Las Cannas to identity his dad, and to observe the scene.

"It was hideous. Shocking beyond belief," he told us. "I listened to what was *said* to have happened, but I will always doubt that the full story wasn't known or being told. I really just don't know. Probably never will."

It has never been proven and as far as we know, the three boys are still in jail. To this very moment, we remain terribly sad by the violent and untimely loss of our friend.

Unbelievably, not a week later, Socorro called to tell us that Los Alisios had been broken into and ransacked. That devastating call was followed soon after by an email from Karen who wrote that she and her husband, when they returned home from an early evening out, had encountered robbers who roughed her up and beat him unconscious. They moved to an in-town apartment and never returned to their home, which was located next to the *barrio* where many of her students lived. The children that she taught . . . and showered with pure and caring love.

*   *   *

Our hearts were heavy with all this news. Could we possibly

return to Cabarete in December, to the uncertainty that would undoubtedly confront us? Add to that, the knifing encounter—*in our home*. Could Bill have had *his* throat slashed, right there in front of me?

It saddened me to realize that just a few episodes by desperate people could scare us away. I understand how people could resent "outsiders" who had the good life in Cabarete, and then went home to continue the good life somewhere else, leaving behind all kinds of things that would make the life of any Dominican family easier and more comfortable. Actually, I don't resent what they took from our house. What I *do* regret is that these episodes of violence have taken away our feeling of safety in Cabarete. But then, what about all the other Dominicans who had enriched our lives in ways that would stay with us forever?

Perhaps if we were younger—

*   *   *

The Lakehouse had always been a place for peaceful reflection on joys, successes, problems, and situations that needed resolution. One tranquil evening on the deck overlooking Merrymeeting Lake, we decided the time had come to close this amazing chapter of our lives.

It wasn't an easy decision. It had been a glorious ride from that first excited phone call from Ann and John twenty years before, to our sweet farewell this past April when the moon over Cabarete beamed down upon us as we sat in our *cabaña*. A score of years we would never regret.

Within the week, we called Gordon. "How would you like to buy Los Alisios," Bill asked, knowing how badly he had wanted beach access for his Windsurf Resort members.

"The check is in the mail," Gordon responded even before we mentioned price. His voice was up a few octaves above norm.

*   *   *

Later that summer, Bill made reservations for the upcoming winter to be spent in the St. Petersburg area of Florida. We missed the exuberant enthusiasm of our flights to the Dominican Republic, restraining ourselves from clapping as we landed.

Now, in 2014, we sit here on our balcony in Florida, overlooking the Gulf Intracoastal Waterway, reaffirming our love and respect for one another, and finalizing this memoir.

Yet, as we look at each other with a glint in our eyes, we are poised and ready, perhaps, for some new adventure to begin with the next cycle of a *Moon Over . . . ?*

"Don't cry because it's over. Smile because it happened."

—Dr. Seuss

Main Street, Cabarete - 2005

CPSIA information can be obtained at www.ICGtesting.com
Printed in the USA
BVOW11s1535071215

429600BV00007B/92/P